CONTENTS.

	PAGE
DEVELOPMENT OF SYSTEMATIC FORESTRY IN EUROPE	6
FORESTRY IN GREAT BRITAIN AND IRELAND	7
FORESTRY IN JAPAN	11
INDIGENOUS INDIAN FORESTRY. SACRED GROVES	12
GAME PRESERVES	13
AJMERE-MERWARA. BEDNOR. HAMIRGARH	14
THE KÁNS OF SORAB	17
GOVERNMENT TIMBER MONOPOLY ON THE WESTERN COAST	19
FOREST MANAGEMENT IN MALABAR AND KANARA	21
NILAMBUR TEAK PLANTATION	23
DR. GIBSON IN BOMBAY, DR. CLEGHORN IN MADRAS	25
THE ATTARAN FORESTS IN TENASSERIM HANDED OVER TO PRIVATE ENTERPRISE	28
MAJOR PHAYRE IN PEGU	29
SYSTEM INITIATED IN 1856	30
PEGU FORESTS THROWN OPEN TO PRIVATE ENTERPRISE	32
CHANGE OF POLICY	34
PLANTATIONS	37
DEMARCATION OF FORESTS. KAREN AREAS	39
YIELD OF FORESTS	40
FOREST ADMINISTRATION IN OTHER PROVINCES	43
PROTECTION OF FORESTS AGAINST FIRE	44
ORGANIZATION OF ESTABLISHMENTS	46
INDIAN FOREST FLORAS	49
FOREST LEGISLATION	51
TANNING MATERIALS, CAOUTCHOUC, IRON	54
CATTLE FODDER	59
EVIL EFFECTS OF DENUDATION	64
THE DEHRA DÙN FOREST SCHOOL	68
WORKING PLANS CONTROLLED BY INSPECTOR-GENERAL OF FORESTS	72

Contents.

	PAGE
THE INCREASE OF POPULATION NECESSITATES GOOD FOREST MANAGEMENT	74
EXTENSION OF CULTIVATION BY RELINQUISHING LAND IN THE REMOTE TIMBER FORESTS	76
PARAMOUNT IMPORTANCE OF MINOR FORESTS AND PASTURE LANDS	77
ESTABLISHMENT OF VILLAGE FORESTS	81
THE DIFFICULTIES OF THE TASK MUST BE FACED	84
NATIVE FOREST OFFICERS MUST BE EMPLOYED IN RESPONSIBLE APPOINTMENTS	85

INDIAN FORESTRY.

A COMPREHENSIVE manual of Forestry in five volumes has now been published by Dr. William Schlich, principal professor of Forestry at the Royal Indian Engineering College, Cooper's Hill, and of the first two volumes a second edition has appeared.* At the same time Mr. Baden-Powell has published a book upon Forest Law.† These two truly excellent publications are the outcome of the efforts made, to introduce in the different provinces of the British Indian Empire a system of regular forest management. Commencing with 1867 young Englishmen have devoted themselves to the study of forestry, and every year a number which has varied, according to the requirements of the service in India, from 4 to 12 have gone out, after undergoing the needful training in their profession, to be employed in the Indian Forest service. These books are the first comprehensive manuals of this subject published in English, and they have placed the professional studies of Candidates for the Indian Forest Service upon a safe and satisfactory footing. Without Forestry in India these books would not have been published.

* A Manual of Forestry, by William Schlich, C.I.E., PH.D.; Vol. I. Introduction to Forestry, second edition, 1896; Vol. II. Practical Sylviculture, 1891; Vol. III. Forest Management, 1895; Vol. IV. Forest Protection (translation of Forstschutz, by Dr. R. Hess), by W. R. Fisher, B.A., 1895; Vol. V. Forest Utilization (translation of Forstbenutzung by Dr. Karl Gayer), by W. R. Fisher, B.A., 1896. London: Bradbury, Agnew and Co.

† Forest Law, by B. H. Baden-Powell, C.I.E., M.A. London: Bradbury, Agnew and Co., 1893.

Development of Systematic Forestry in Europe.

Systematic Forestry, all over the world, is a profession of comparatively recent origin. In most countries of Europe it has been the result of the rapid growth of population within the last 250 years, but other circumstances, besides the increase of population, have influenced its development. As long as towns, villages, and the cultivated area surrounding them, were confined to the fertile lands in the plains and in the river valleys, the forests on the hills and on broken or less fertile ground, yielded sufficient timber, fuel and other produce for the requirements of the agricultural and town populations. Where the forest area was sufficiently extensive, it satisfied all requirements without material injury to its productiveness. As cultivation extended, and as the forest area was diminished, systematic treatment became a necessity and the consequence was, that gradually woodlands came to be managed like gardens, fields, meadows or other landed estates.

In most parts of Central Europe, particularly in Germany and France, the old system of management was different according to the prevailing species. On lands stocked with Oak, Beech, Birch, Hornbeam and other broad-leaved trees, the regeneration of the forest was effected, to some extent from self-sown seedlings, to a larger extent from coppice shoots. We have historical evidence, that in parts of Germany forests of this description were managed during the 15th century in a systematic and rational manner. These woodlands were divided into a certain number of blocks, corresponding to the years of rotation adopted for the underwood. At each cutting of the underwood most of the older standards were removed, while the younger standards were left. To this day such a system, greatly improved, of coppice under standards, is maintained over large areas in Germany, it is the principal system, under which private proprietors in central and northern France manage their woods of broad-leaved trees, and the Oak-woods of Sussex and other counties of South England are treated in the same manner. High forests on the other hand of Beech and Oak, but particularly of coniferous trees, of Spruce, Silver Fir and Scotch Pine, have from time immemorial been worked on the principle of cutting out the trees wanted for immediate use, and relying upon self-sown seedlings for their regeneration. This practice of cutting trees here and there, to meet the requirements of the moment, answered well, where the forests were extensive and the demands limited. When however the requirements of Iron mines, of salt works, of glass factories and other industrial establishments assumed large proportions, when the timber trade expanded, and enormous numbers of logs were wanted to be floated, bound up in huge rafts, down the Rhine and other large rivers, it became necessary to make clearances upon a large scale and the necessity of arranging the cuttings according to a well-considered system became obvious. In the various parts of Germany this system has developed in a different manner, different according to species, mode of transport and other circumstances. This development commenced in the 16th century and has continued steadily to the present day. The history of the changes which the treatment of high forest has gradually undergone in Germany, is most interesting and instructive, but it would be impossible to set it forth on the present occasion.

In France an important step in advance was made, when in 1669, Colbert, the great Finance Minister of Louis Quatorze, issued his famous "ordonnance," which among other things gave instructions concerning the treatment of high forests. The present excellent treatment, however, of high forests belonging to the State in France, has mainly been built upon the systems gradually worked out in Germany.

Forestry in Great Britain and Ireland.

In Great Britain and Ireland certain branches of sylviculture are well understood, plantations are made with great skill and at a very moderate outlay per acre, osier beds and coppice woods for raising hop poles, as a rule are very successful. But the treatment of high forests has in no way developed in the same manner as in Germany, France, and, at a later period, in other countries on the Continent of Europe. It is a fact, that under existing circumstances in Great Britain home-grown timber cannot compete with imported timber, for the simple reason, that from the beginning it has not received proper treatment. The trees stand too far apart, thinnings are much too heavy, hence the woods are open and the result is seen in short, knotty and branched boles. There are exceptions, but open, park-like woods are the rule, and these do not yield timber of first-rate quality. Another reason, why timber traders prefer imported timber, is that home-grown timber is thrown upon the market in an irregular manner. All at once heavy cuttings are made, to provide money, or for other reasons, and then perhaps nothing is cut in the same district for years to come. On the other hand, timber of the exact description required by the market is imported regularly at the principal ports of the United Kingdom, no wonder therefore that the timber trader prefers this source of supply, because it enables him to satisfy his customers at the right time. There is no help for it, if the market is to be supplied with home-grown timber, woods must be treated differently, and well-considered systems of management must be introduced, whereby a regular annual supply of first-class timber in each district shall be assured.

The reason for this state of things is not far to seek. In Germany, when the country was recovering, very slowly, from the devastation, which the thirty years' war had wrought, the steady increase of the population caused serious apprehensions, lest the supply of fuel should fail, and this apprehension of necessity led to systematic forest management. In Great Britain, when fuel became less plentiful, the inexhaustible supplies of coal and peat came in to meet the demand. And while in Germany the treatment of high forests, the thinning of young woods and the successive cutting of mature trees, has been brought to a high state of perfection by patient research and systematic experiment, the timber requirements of Great Britain have always been readily supplied by sea with the best material from all parts of the world. And there has been another circumstance. Great Britain has never been devastated by a calamity like the thirty years' war in Germany, which put a stop to the accumulation of wealth, that, in spite of most imperfect means of communication, had commenced in the middle ages. In the German Empire more than 16 million acres, $47\frac{1}{2}\%$ of the entire Forest area, are at present owned by private proprietors. Speaking broadly, the wealth, such as it is, of these landowners, large and small, only consists in the land. Sheer necessity therefore compels them, to make the most of it and to manage their woodlands upon correct principles.

In Great Britain, on the other hand, the steady uninterrupted accumulation of wealth during many centuries, and the enormous value of town lands, has made the families of most landed proprietors to a great extent independent of the income derived from fields, meadows and woodlands. They can afford the luxury of huge parks, in the management of which the preservation of game and æsthetic considerations are foremost. Yet, even in Great Britain, the decline in the price of wheat and other agricultural produce is making itself felt here and there among landed proprietors, their income has diminished, and in many cases it would be desirable to increase that income. In that portion of his Manual,* which deals with Forestry in Great Britain and Ireland, Dr. Schlich draws attention to the fact, that a large portion of the timber and other forest produce at present imported, might be produced in the United Kingdom, if the existing woodlands were managed in a more systematic manner, and if their area were increased by planting up waste lands. He shows that the mean annual imports of timber and minor forest produce during the years 1890-94

* Volume I., second edition, p. 101.

were valued at £26,592,000, and that they are increasing steadily. Teak, Mahogany and other furniture woods, Cork, Gum, Caoutchouc, Gutta Percha and other minor forest produce, the value of which is included in these figures, could of course not be produced in the United Kingdom, but Oak, Fir and wood pulp could easily be grown. The value of these imported articles, Dr. Schlich shows, amounts to £17,916,000 a year, and this quantity, he believes, might, under good management, be produced in the United Kingdom on 6 million acres. Dr. Schlich also shows, from official returns, that woodlands and plantations in Great Britain and Ireland, measure 3 million acres, rough pasture lands 12½ millions, and that there is a large extent of unclassed surplus, comprising, besides inland water, turf bogs, marshes and barren mountain land, which aggregates 14¼ million acres. The rough pasture lands yield rent as sheepwalks or are let for shooting, but most of the area here mentioned produces none or only insignificant returns. At first sight it would seem to be out of the question, that any timber grown upon this area should compete with imported timber, unless indeed heavy duties were levied upon the imported article. In Scandinavia, Russia, Germany and France wages are much lower than in Great Britain, and these countries furnish 60 per cent. of the imported timber. The imposition of import duties however Dr. Schlich does not contemplate. The production of timber, he explains, demands comparatively little labour, forests require one-tenth to one-twentieth only of the labour necessary for land under field crops.* Climate and soil are more powerful factors than wages, in regulating the cost of timber production, and these factors are singularly favourable in Great Britain and Ireland. Hence he is able to show that at present wages and timber prices the annual net rental of average land, planted with Scotch Pine and larch, and treated under a rotation of 100 years, amounts to 7s. 6d. per acre, the entire outlay being charged with compound

---

* Volume I., second edition, p. 25.

interest at the rate of 2½ per cent. All land therefore, which does not now yield a rent of 7s. 6d. per acre, may, if suitable, be profitably planted. These are very important facts, and those pages of Dr. Schlich's manual, in which these facts are set forth, as well as many other portions of that excellent work, might usefully be studied by landed proprietors, wood managers and foresters, as well as by estate agents in the United Kingdom.

The preceding remarks concerning the development of forestry as a scientific profession on the Continent of Europe and its possible development in the United Kingdom may serve better to explain some points in connection with the development of forestry in India.

Forestry in Japan.

The only country outside Europe, where some system of forestry has grown up independently of European methods, is Japan. It would lead too far upon the present occasion, to enter into detail, but so much may be said, that the woodlands in the plains and on the lower hills, which are well stocked with coniferous trees, chiefly with Sugi (Cryptomeria japonica) and Hinoki (Chamæcyparis obtusa) furnish all the building material used in the Empire.* In his excellent work on Japan, Rein designates these forests as cultivated woods (Cultur wälder), and he thinks that they have all been artificially raised.† The Japanese believe that on the island of Nippon such forests were raised 1200 years ago. The area of these woodlands aggregates upwards of 13 million acres (18% of the total area of the Empire). On the mountains of Japan however there is no trace of any old system of forestry. Of late years however the Japanese Government have sent a number of young men to Germany for their professional training in forestry, and with the aid of a few German foresters from Bavaria, a regular Forest Department has been organized in that country.

* Charles Sprague Sargent, Forest Flora of Japan, 1894, p. 85.
† Rein, Japan, Vol. II., 1886, p. 255.

Indigenous Indian Forestry. Sacred Groves.

In India, with the exception of small beginnings chiefly in Rajputana, of which a brief account will be given further on, the preservation of sacred groves, and of woodlands as game preserves, has been the only attempt formerly made in this direction.

Very little has been published regarding sacred groves in India, but they are, or rather were, very numerous. I have found them in nearly all provinces. As instances I may mention the Garo and Khasia hills which I visited in 1879, the Devara Kadus or sacred groves of Coorg with which I became acquainted in 1868, and the hill ranges of the Salem district in the Madras Presidency examined by me in 1882. Well known are the Swami Shola on the Yelagiris, the sacred grove at Pudúr on the Javadis and several sacred forests on the Shevaroys.* These are situated in the moister parts of the country. In the dry region sacred groves are particularly numerous in Rajputana. In Mewar they usually consist of Anogeissus pendula, a moderate sized tree with small leaves, which fall early in the dry season, in December and January. Before falling the foliage of these trees turns a beautiful yellowish red, and at that season these woods resemble our Beech forests in autumn. In the southernmost States of Rajputana, in Partabgarh and Banswara, in a somewhat moister climate, the sacred groves, here called Malwan, consist of a variety of trees, Teak among the number. These sacred forests, as a rule, are never touched by the axe, except when wood is wanted for the repair of religious buildings, or in special cases for other purposes.

A remarkable little forest of Sál (Shorea robusta) I found in 1864 near Gorakhpur in the Northwest provinces. A German Missionary, of the Church Missionary Society, who then had a large congregation of Native Christians, introduced me to a Muhammedan Saint, belonging to a

* Brandis, Suggestions regarding Forest Administration in the Madras Presidency, Madras, 1883, p. 173.

peculiar sect, who maintained, in the courtyard of the building which he inhabited, a perpetual fire, fed with huge pieces of Sál timber. These he obtained from a forest in the vicinity of the town, which I visited. The forest was in good condition, and well protected. Nothing was allowed to be cut, except the wood required to feed the sacred fire, and this required the cutting annually of a small number of trees which were carefully selected among those that showed signs of age and decay. The Saint was known all over the country as Mian Sahib, the Right Reverend Gentleman. He was most liberal minded and was on friendly terms with the Missionary, whose schools he helped to support. In 1857 Gorakhpur had for a considerable period been in the possession of the Mutineers, and during the whole of those troubled times he was able to protect a number of native Christians with their families, who had remained at Gorakhpur, and who had sought shelter in the buildings which he occupied.

Game Preserves.

Game preserves have been established and maintained by native Chiefs in many parts of India, particularly where the climate is dry, and woodlands are scarce. The most extensive of these were the forests of Babul (Acacia arabica) in lower Sind. These were narrow strips of land along the banks of the river Indus, from a quarter of a mile to two miles in breadth. They were established by the Amirs of Sind and were surrounded by walls made of sun-dried bricks. On the annexation of Sind in February 1843 these game preserves became State property and now form the most valuable portion of the State Forests in that province.

In Rajputana I found in December 1869 and January 1870, on a march from Agra to Guzerat, that in the States of Bhartpur, Jaipur, Mewar (Udaipur) Kishangarh, Partabgarh and Banswara, as well as on the estates of the great feudal nobles in some of these territories, the custom prevailed, to preserve large areas of forest and grass lands, to furnish cover for game, and a permanent supply of grass, wood and timber. Under certain restrictions these preserves were generally open to the surrounding population. As an instance I may mention, that in the large Ghana which is close to the town of Bhartpur, and which at that time covered an area of 40 square miles, any one was allowed to cut dry wood. A certain class of poor people made a regular living by collecting firewood and selling it in the town. The ghana was in charge of a faujdar, who had a guard of 100 sepoys to watch it. It supplied grass for the cattle, horses and elephants of the Raj, and 200 maunds of firewood were brought in from it daily for the different Departments of the State as well as for the workshops. It also yielded timber (Nim and Babul) as might be required. Besides the Bhartpur ghana, there were at that time in the State four other preserves, maintained for similar purposes, aggregating 42 square miles. In the small State of Kishangarh I found two preserves, one near the capital of the same name, the other near the town of Rupnagar. The last, which I visited on 21st December, is situated four miles south of the town on a low range of hills about 3 miles long and half a mile wide. As a rule only the cattle of the Raj were allowed to graze here, and large quantities of grass were cut and stored. But during the years of drought and famine, in 1867 and 1868, shortly before my visit, the cattle of Rupnagar were allowed to graze here, the branches of trees were allowed to be cut for cattle fodder, and I found many trees of Khejri (Prosopis spicigera) thus lopped. The same had been done in Kishangarh and a large proportion of the cattle of these two places were thus fed and preserved during those terrible years.

Ajmere-Merwara. Bednor. Hamirgarh.

The indirect advantages also of forest protection in the dry climate of Rajputana were appreciated by some of the landed proprietors. In the British districts of Ajmere and

Merwara the whole of the waste and jungle, situated in Government villages, had at the settlement of 1850 been handed over to the inhabitants, the Government relinquishing its rights in these lands. The practical result of this policy, dictated though it was by the highest motives, was disastrous. The hills and other waste lands had become denuded, the wood was used, what timber there was had been sold, and these lands were for the most part utterly barren. During the drought of 1867 and 1868 all grass on these naked hillsides dried up, the cattle perished or had to be driven away.

For their crops the inhabitants of these districts almost entirely depend upon irrigation. The water is furnished by numerous tanks formed by embankments thrown across valleys at convenient points. Many of these tanks are old, others have been built since the country has been under British rule. Colonel Dixon, who for many years governed these districts, and whose name on my visits in 1869 and 1878 was remembered with gratitude by the people, had repaired the old tanks, and had built many new ones. The scanty rainfall in these districts does not come down continuously, but in a small number of heavy showers, which rush down the barren hillsides in torrents, and instead of filling the tanks slowly but steadily, are apt to break the bunds, or fill them with the silt which their scour has brought down. These districts I visited on my journey in December, 1869. The cattle had perished, the people had fled, large villages were entirely deserted, and the country was almost depopulated by these years of drought and famine. Of many tanks I found the embankments forming the tank had been breached by sudden floods, others had silted up completely. Coming from Todgarh on 1st January, 1870, I entered the territory of the Thakur of Bednor, a Feudatory to the Maharajah of Udaipur, and the contrast in the appearance of the country greatly surprised me. In British territory the hills, which at one time had been covered by a fair Jungle of Khair (Acacia Catechu) and

Dhaukra (Anogcissus pendula) were denuded, the trees having been sold to the charcoal contractors of the British Cantonment of Nasirabad. Here and there an isolated useless tree of Saler (Boswellia) remained, showing the height which the original wood had attained. As soon however as I entered the territory of Bednor, the hills were wooded, not a tree having been felled. The Thakur's eldest son, who at that time had the management of the estate, accompanied me on the 2d January through his forests. From the top of Bairat hill we looked down upon the town, with its large tank and beautiful groves of fruit trees, and there he told me, how the Nasirabad charcoal contractors had come repeatedly, offering large sums if he would allow them to cut. He had refused and would always refuse their request, knowing well that the grass, which, even in dry seasons, maintained itself under the shade of the trees, and the branches of the trees themselves, had saved the cattle of Bednor in years of drought, and more than this, that the water supply in those tanks, upon which the fertility of the country depended, was maintained by the forest growth upon the hills.

A little further south, in the estates of another Nobleman, the Rao of Hamirgarh, I had the pleasure of examining woodlands managed on something approaching a regular system. On 5th January the Rao called upon me at my camp and accompanied me over the whole of his forests, covering a range of hills skirting the Bunass river, 5 miles long and about 2 miles wide. These woods were preserved for shooting, and to furnish grass and wood. Formerly a good deal of wood was made into charcoal to smelt iron, but the iron smelters had left and at the time of my visit there was no smelting. The clearances however had here been made, not promiscuously, but blocks had been cut over successively in a rough kind of rotation, the coppice on the clearances was protected, and was springing up vigorously. It gave the Rao great pleasure when I complimented him upon this attempt at regular management.

The Káns of Sorab.

It is here the place to mention those remarkable woodlands, known as Káns, which are found in the moist districts of the Mysore State, the Malnád, particularly in Shimoga, and which are most frequent in the Taluk of Sorab, adjoining the British districts of North Kanara and Dharwar in the Bombay Presidency. These Káns are patches of dense forest, sharply demarcated from the surrounding country, consisting mainly of evergreen trees, and they are only found within a certain distance from the edge of the Ghats. I examined them in April 1868, on a tour which I made through Mysore. That part of the country is well cultivated, and what forest is left on the hills is deciduous, the chief trees being Terminalia, Lagerstroemia, Pterocarpus, with an underwood of Bamboo. Here and there however there are these patches of evergreen forest varying in size, which are carefully fire traced, so as to keep out the fires of the hot season. They are mostly private property and pay land-tax. In these woods an abundance of the Sago palm, Caryota urens, is found. It springs up readily from self sown seed and grows well under the shade of the large trees, which constitute the forest. The cut flower stalks yield large quantities of sweet sap, which is either boiled down into sugar, or fermented and made into palm wine. Another product of these woods is black pepper. Like the Caryota, the Pepper vine (Piper nigrum) grows wild here, but is also multiplied by planting. To enable the vine to twine comfortably round the stems, the side branches of the trees are lopped and the underwood from time to time is cleared away. The third produce of these Káns is Jack fruit, the tree (Artocarpus integrifolia) being plentiful. In some of these woods in the southern portion of the Shimoga district I found coffee trees cultivated. Besides the three principal kinds of produce named, these Káns also yield fuel, wood for building, branches and leaves, to manure paddy fields,

Areca nut plantations and Betel gardens. It has already been stated, that these Káns vary in size. The largest examined by me was the Korkáni Kán near Sorab, six miles long and about 3 miles wide. Of this however one third only was at that time occupied and assessed. Another Kán near Sorab measured 300 acres. Most of the Káns are situated on high ground, and although the people expressed the opinion, that they were generally on better soil, this did not accord with the conclusions I formed at the time. Soil and position of the Káns near Sorab seemed to me to be similar to the dry forest in the vicinity. They do not extend further east than about 30 miles from the edge of the ghats, and they are not found in the dry maidan country of Mysore. Káns are said also to occur in North Kanara above the ghats, and to be used for rearing the pepper vine. In Hunter's Imperial Gazetteer, second edition, vol. xiii., page 65, it is said: "These Káns are caused by corresponding depressions in the substratum of laterite, which permit a surface soil of great depth to gather; whereas over the rest of the country the mould is only about 4 inches deep." This view of the case, which agrees with the local opinion previously stated may be correct, but so much seems certain, that the Káns are maintained in their present condition chiefly through protection from the annual jungle fires. Were fire allowed to enter, the deciduous trees would soon get the upper hand, pepper, the Sago Palm, and the Jack fruit would certainly disappear, since they can only thrive in the uniformly moist air of these evergreen woods, in the same way as the Betel vine (Piper Betle) demands, besides watering, the shade of trees or the protection of mats whereby the air, in which it grows, is kept sufficiently moist.

So far regarding old and indigenous attempts at Forestry in India. The second and more important portion of the present paper will deal with the attempts made by the British Government to introduce a regular system of forest management.

Government Timber Monopoly on the Western Coast.

The first attempt at Forest management was a great mistake, an act of injustice which cannot be condemned too severely. Originally started, in order to secure a permanent supply, it degenerated into the attempt to establish, without regard to private rights, a Government monopoly of timber. The districts of Malabar and Kanara on the west coast of the peninsula were ceded to the British Government in March 1792 by the treaty, which terminated the second Mysore war. At first these districts were placed under the Government of Bombay and their wealth in Teak timber at once attracted the attention of that Government. In August 1800* the Court of Directors authorized the Bombay Government, to assume the right of felling timber on behalf of the East India Company. These districts having meanwhile been transferred to the Presidency of Fort St. George, the Court's instructions remained some time without effect. It was however arranged, that, while the administration of the country was subordinate to the Government of Madras, the forests should remain under the control of the Government of Bombay, as the timber was required for the Navy and for the shipbuilding industry at Bombay. In 1806 an Officer was appointed Conservator of Forests and in 1807 a proclamation was issued, asserting the Company's right of sovereignty over the forests, and forbidding the felling of timber by private individuals. Undoubtedly the object of the Court of Directors in issuing their orders of 1800 was, to receive a regular supply of timber for public purposes from the public forests, to which alone the proclamation was intended to apply. The Conservator of Forests however assumed much larger powers, and apparently he was supported by the Government to which he was subordinate. Commissioners of Survey, it is true, had been appointed by the

* Summary of papers relating to the Madras and Bombay Forests in Selections from the Records of the Bengal Government, IX. Calcutta, 1852, p. 177.

Bombay Government, to ascertain the limits of what might be considered public forests, but no attempt was made to settle the boundaries of these public forests, and to demarcate them. In Malabar, as well as in some of the adjoining parts of Kanara, most of the land had from time immemorial been in the possession of large proprietors, who claimed proprietary rights over the forests as well as over cultivated lands. Tippoo Sahib, the Sultan of Mysore, however, had, while he ruled these districts, in an arbitrary manner set aside these rights, particularly the right of felling timber, which he claimed as a Royal privilege. The Sultan's action was supposed to justify the proceedings of the Bombay Government and its Officers. The Conservator of Forests extended his operations over the whole country, he cut down and appropriated to the use of the Government, not only the trees of the private forests, but even those growing on cultivated lands. The proprietor was compelled to pay duty on the timber growing upon his own property, when he made use of it for his own purposes. Finally, in order to prevent shipbuilding by pirates on the coasts of Persia and Arabia, all exportation of timber by sea was prohibited, and thus the trade in timber was almost annihilated. For the regeneration and improvement of the forests the Conservator did nothing. The system was one of oppressive monopoly. It was complained of by all the local authorities, by the Judges, the Magistrates and the Collectors. In 1822 Sir Thomas Munro, then Governor of Madras, insisted on its being abolished. The minute[*] which he recorded upon this subject is a model of clear and powerful reasoning. "In order to protect the property of the public and of individuals, their limits must first be ascertained, and this can only be done by a survey," and further on: "The people now submit reluctantly to our monopoly, but we should recollect, that no paltry profit in timber can compensate for the loss of their good will."

[*] Major-General Sir Thomas Munro, Bart., K.C.B., by Sir Alexander Arbuthnot, Vol. I., London, 1881, p. 178.

The appointment of Conservator of Forests having been abolished, it would seem, that Government, as has often been the case in India, went from one extreme into the other. No steps were taken to define the limits of the public forests and the forest rights of Government remained in abeyance. Indeed, 54 years later, in 1876, the Madras Government passed orders which would have led to the abandonment of all forest rights of Government in South Kanara. This however fortunately was prevented by the Government of India.

Forest Management in Malabar and Kanara.

It was only after the Madras Forest Act had been passed in 1882, that real progress was made in the direction indicated by Sir Thomas Munro. The limits of the public forests were ascertained by careful enquiry on the spot, claims to rights of occupancy and of user within those areas were invited, and such rights, as had been proved, were either bought out, liberal compensation in land or money being given, or, if this could not be done, the continued exercise of these rights within the forest was authorized. It will readily be understood that the establishment of a just and equitable procedure in this difficult business constituted a new departure in the administration of the public forests. The procedure pursued since then in the Madras Presidency as well as, from an earlier date, in all other parts of the British Indian Empire, was framed on the same principles, which have regulated forest legislation in France and Germany. From the commencement it was agreed that long continued user in the public forests should be regarded as constituting a right, and that in the settlement of forests these rights should be dealt with in the same manner as in Europe. The result has been, that in the districts of Malabar and Kanara considerable areas have been constituted Reserved Forests, which is the term corresponding in India to what on the continent of Europe we call State Forests. In 1862 a portion of Kanara, known under the name of North Kanara, was replaced under the authority of the Bombay Government; in the following remarks therefore North Kanara will be dealt with separately.

On 30 June 1895 the area of reserved forests in Malabar amounted to 121,676 acres, and in South Kanara to 72,795 acres. In neither district has the work of demarcation and settlement been completed, for there are still large areas of reserved lands,* (Government lands reserved from alienation,) a portion of which will probably be added to the reserved forests, when their settlement comes to be completed. The area of these reserved lands in Malabar in 1895 amounted to 265,000 and in South Kanara to 656,000 acres. In Malabar the area of reserved forests is $3\frac{1}{2}$ and in Kanara 3 per cent. of the entire area of the district. Even if further proceedings should have the result of doubling this area, the percentage would be a very small one. It has already been explained, that in Malabar as well as in a portion of South Kanara a considerable proportion of the forest is claimed by large proprietors. Nevertheless there were extensive tracts formerly not thus claimed, and it is now acknowledged generally, that if the work of demarcation and settlement had been taken in hand at an earlier date, the area of reserved forests would be much larger. As population increases, the forests are more largely resorted to by the people to supply their requirements, rights of user spring up, and the area that can be obtained as State Forest necessarily diminishes annually.

In the Bombay Presidency another Forest Law, the Indian Forest Act of 1878 is in force, and under the provisions of that Act two classes of forests have been constituted : reserved forests and protected forests. The procedure in the demarcation and settlement of reserved forests is the same as in the Madras Presidency, protected forests in some respects correspond to reserved lands, but there is a difference, into which it would take too long to enter on the present occasion. The total area of North

* The term used officially, though not adopted in the Act.

Kanara amounts to 3,910 square miles, and of this area there were in 1894 no less than 1,182 square miles (756,500 acres) of Reserved Forests, or 30 % of the total area. In addition there are 2,367 square miles of protected forests. North Kanara is a thinly inhabited forest country with only 114 souls on the square mile, while South Kanara has 271 and Malabar 475. The larger State Forest area however is chiefly due to the circumstance, that ever since the district was transferred to Bombay and some time previously, while it was under Madras, great attention had been paid to the protection of the forests, and this has much facilitated the work of forest settlement. This large area of forest in North Kanara will amply repay the labour bestowed upon it. Some of the most valuable Teak localities of India are here, they are now being protected against fire and the cutting of timber is regulated by well-considered working plans.

Nilambur Teak Plantation.

A most satisfactory feature in the Madras portion of these western districts is, that in 1844 the then Collector, Mr. Conolly, commenced establishing Teak plantations upon a large scale near Nilambur in Malabar. The object, which this public spirited Officer had in view, was "to replace those forests which had vanished from private carelessness and rapacity." Doubtless the Court of Directors and the Government of Bombay had originally been guided by the idea, that the interest of private proprietors could not be depended upon for efficient measures to assure a permanent supply of timber. But Government, while over-riding in an arbitrary manner the rights of private proprietors, had done nothing, during a period of 22 years, to assure a permanent supply by properly managing and improving the forests. Nor had anything been done either by Government, or by private proprietors during a second period, from 1822 to 1844. Conolly determined to raise Teak forests on a large scale on Government account.

This undertaking he justly designated as : "a work too new, too extensive and too barren of early return to be ever taken up by the native proprietor." At the outset two difficulties presented themselves. The first difficulty was, to obtain the land upon which to plant. Mr. Conolly had selected for his operations the valley of the Nilambur river, which runs into the sea at the port of Beypur, and is connected by a navigable canal with the town of Calicut, the principal timber market on the western coast. The greater part of the land however in this valley belonged to the Nilambur Rajah, a wealthy landowner, who was not prepared to part with any of his land. Fortunately one of the many religious bodies holding temple-lands happened to be in want of funds. Thus a considerable area was obtained, which was subsequently, by other purchases, increased to nearly 19,000 acres. The second difficulty was to get the Teak seed to germinate. The structure of the Teak seed is peculiar. Surrounded by an enlarged and inflated bladder-like calyx is a thick spongy mass which encloses the nut, the seeds being protected by a thick and excessively hard bony shell. Teak timber being extremely valuable, holding the place so to say which gold holds among metals, and the diamond among precious stones, the seed had long attracted the attention of the people on the western coast of the peninsula as well as in Burma. Mr. Conolly was told, that in the natural forests the outer covering of the seed was destroyed by the jungle fires of the hot season, that this was necessary to enable the seed to germinate, and attempts were actually made to effect this object, by covering the seed with a light coating of dry grass and setting fire to it. Another advice was to plunge the seed in water nearly boiling. All these dodges were of no avail, but here as elsewhere the simplest plan succeeded best, plenty of water under a light covering of earth and leaves.

Mr. Conolly commenced his experiments in 1842, and in 1844 he had raised 50,000 healthy seedlings, which were planted out on deep alluvial soil near the river. These plantations were extended steadily, first at the rate of 100 acres a year, afterwards more slowly. In 1878 the area planted up aggregated 3,436 acres, and the oldest compartments, which at that time were on an average 33 years old, were stocked with a dense wood of Teak poles nearly 100 feet high. These poles find a ready market at Calicut, some areas therefore have been cleared and replanted, and of late years a species of mahogany (Swietenia macrophylla) has been introduced as a mixture, a move in the right direction, for Teak thrives best when growing in company with other trees.

At a later date, a few years before North Kanara was handed back to Bombay, planting of Teak in that district also was commenced under the direction of Dr. Cleghorn, at that time Conservator of Forests in the Madras Presidency. These operations were continued by the Bombay forest officers, and in 1894 the Teak plantations in this district aggregated 1,584 acres.

Dr. Gibson in Bombay, Dr. Cleghorn in Madras.

To the Governments of Bombay and Madras belongs the credit of having been the first to organize a regular administration of the public forests within the territories under their control. The Officers selected to fill the post of Conservator of Forests in these two Presidencies were medical men, Dr. Alexander Gibson, who was appointed in 1847, and Dr. Hugh Cleghorn, who became Conservator of Forests of Madras in 1856. Both were Botanists, they were good men of business, and they have done much to promote Indian forestry. Before however Dr. Cleghorn was appointed Conservator, measures had been taken to work the Anamalay forests in the Coimbatore district, which at that time were rich in large and valuable Teak timber.

The Teak tree is only found in the moister districts of tropical India and Burma, but it is by no means limited to the coast districts below Ghat, Malabar and Kanara. Indeed in that portion of Malabar which is situated above Ghat, in Wainád, are some Teak forests, which, before they were cleared out of all mature timber, were extremely valuable. And in North Kanara the most extensive and most valuable Teak producing tracts are the Sonda forests on the edge of the Deccan. The Anamalay forests are another instance of valuable Teak producing tracts situated above the line of Ghats. The timber from these is exported in both directions, to the coast and to the inland districts of the Karnatik. In order to work these forests, Lieutenant (now Major-General) James Michael was appointed in June 1848. He organized the cutting and transport of the timber, he brought about a lease of valuable forests from a large landowner, the Nambadi of Colengode, and he started a system of clearing Teak seedlings and young Teak trees in the forests, of dry leaves and other inflammable matter, so as to protect them against injury by the annual fires of the dry season.

About the time that Michael commenced work in the Anamalay forests, Dr. Cleghorn was stationed as an Assistant Surgeon at Shimoga in Mysore, which State at that time was under British administration. He remarked the wholesale destruction of the forests through the system of shifting cultivation by clearing and burning, known as Kumri. It was mainly through his representations, that the attention of the Commissioner of Mysore was drawn to the necessity of forest conservancy. Kumri cultivation was stopped, and in 1868, while on a tour of inspection through Mysore, I had the satisfaction of seeing large tracts of country clothed with dense young forest which had grown up on the old Kumri clearings.

In those days the destruction of forests in India had attracted the attention of scientific men at home. In 1850 the British Association for the Advancement of Science, at their meeting in Edinburgh, appointed a Committee to consider the probable effects, in an economical and physical point of view, of the destruction of tropical forests. The members of that committee were : Dr. Hugh Cleghorn, Professor Forbes Royle, Captain R. Baird Smith, Captain (now General) R. Strachey. The report was presented to the Ipswich meeting of the Association in 1851. It was drawn up by Dr. Cleghorn, and contributed much to induce public men, seriously to consider the necessity of organizing Forest conservancy in India.

While Dr. Cleghorn was Conservator of forests in Madras, the Government of that Presidency prohibited, by an order of May 1860, Kumri cultivation in Government Forests without previous permission, and directed, that this permission should be given sparingly and never for spots in the timber forests. This point Dr. Cleghorn was able to carry, as he had helped to bring it about 13 years previously with the Government of Mysore, because he was known to be a true friend of the natives, he entertained feelings of warm sympathy towards them, and had made himself familiar with their mode of life and system of husbandry.

At a later period Kumri was again permitted in Mysore, and in Madras the beneficial effect of the order of 1860 has to a great extent been rendered nugatory by the tendency, which subsequently prevailed in that Presidency, to regard as private property a large portion of the forest lands, that had formerly been considered to be the property of Government. It was not until the Madras Forest Act of 1882 was passed, that these matters were finally settled in a satisfactory manner. This Act was passed while the Right Honble. Sir Mountstuart E. Grant Duff was Governor of that Presidency. The good, which that Statesman accomplished in an unobtrusive manner in Madras, has never been sufficiently acknowledged. The Forest Department was reorganized and has since made fairly good progress. In the Civil Department he quietly, but with firmness, broke through the system of promotion by seniority, which had earned for the Southern Presidency the name of the " Benighted."

The Attaran Forests in Tenasserim handed over to Private Enterprise.

On the east side of the Bay of Bengal the Tenasserim provinces had in 1826 been ceded to the British Government at the end of the first Burmese war. In 1827 Dr. Nathaniel Wallich, Superintendent of the Botanical Garden at Calcutta, was directed to enquire into the resources of the country in regard both to botanical science as well as military and commercial objects. In his Report upon the Attaran forests he wrote : " No forest exists which can with propriety be called inexhaustible—at least none that is liable to constant and extensive demands for timber. Private enterprise " (if the forests are thrown open) " will soon render fruitless all endeavours to perpetuate the supplies for the public service."*

On Dr. Wallich's suggestion an attempt on a small scale was made, to work the Attaran forests on Government account, this attempt having resulted in a loss of 250 Rupees, the Government decided to throw open the forest to private enterprise. The result has been as Dr. Wallich had predicted. In 1846 the then Commissioner, Captain (afterwards Sir Henry) Durand, had determined to resume the forests and to work them on Government account, as the rules under which the forests had been thrown open, had been utterly disregarded by the lessees. The Maulmain timber merchants, who formed the bulk of the local Residents, protested, and being supported by the Calcutta Press, the Government of India gave way.† Mr. John Russell Colvin was sent to succeed Captain Durand, the Attaran forests were relinquished, but care was taken to retain in the hands of Government the Thoungyeen and some other more remote forests.

* Summary of papers relating to the Tenasserim Forests in Selections from the Records of the Bengal Government, IX., Calcutta, 1852, p. 77.
† John Russell Colvin, by Sir Auckland Colvin, Oxford, 1895, p. 151.

Major Phayre in Pegu.

In December 1852, at the close of the second Burmese war, the province of Pegu was annexed to the British Indian Empire. Lord Dalhousie, at that time Governor-General of India, had selected the very best man for the government of the newly acquired province, Major (afterwards Sir Arthur) Phayre. Dr. McClelland, like Gibson and Cleghorn a Medical Officer, who had done distinguished service in Assam, in starting, in company with Dr. Wallich and Dr. Griffith, the first Tea plantation on Government account, was appointed Superintendent of Forests. After two years of hard work, exploring the forests and endeavouring to work them, he resigned his post, and in January 1856 the writer was appointed to succeed him. On landing in Calcutta in December 1855, I had the good fortune at once to meet Dr. McClelland and thus to make myself acquainted with the leading features of the task that was before me. The main objects which I had fixed upon as my aim were threefold : (1) To protect and, as far as possible, to improve the forests, to arrange the cuttings so as to keep well within their productive powers, in order to ensure a permanent and sustained yield. (2) To make the inhabitants of the forests and the people in the vicinity my friends and allies. (3) As soon as possible to produce an annual surplus revenue. These ideas I had the honour of submitting to His Excellency. Lord Dalhousie listened with great attention, and when I had concluded, he said : " Dr. Brandis, if you succeed in carrying out these excellent plans, you will confer a lasting benefit upon the people of Pegu. I hope you may succeed, and you will have my full support in the matter. I hold it to be the duty of the Government of India to preserve the forest resources of Pegu, and not to allow them to be wasted, as the forest resources of other provinces have been wasted. Unfortunately I must leave India soon, but I trust that my successors will take the same view as myself of the Pegu forests. Should it however thus happen, that at any time the Government of India were not fully alive to the necessity of preserving the forest resources of Pegu, I hope that you will remember what I have told you." Lord Dalhousie left India in March 1856 and died in 1860.

Pegu in 1856 was a thinly inhabited country. The population at that time is not accurately known, but may safely be estimated at 700,000 souls on 33,195 Square miles, corresponding to 21 on the Square mile. Although population has since then increased in a most wonderful manner, owing chiefly to the wisdom and determination of the first Commissioner, Major Phayre, the census of 1891 only gives 95* on the Square mile, less than the district of North Kanara previously mentioned.

System initiated in 1856.

In 1856 more than 90 per cent. of the province was forest. At annexation the Teak forests had, by proclamation, been declared the property of the State, and this was in accordance with old established custom, for under the King of Burma Teak had been a royalty, all Teak trees were the property of the King and Teak timber was a monopoly. So far the position of Government was clear, but I knew, that in order to have actual control, it was necessary, to keep all operations in the forests in my own hands. Hence I determined to bring out the timber on Government account, to sell it by public auction at Rangoon, and in order to enable me to do this, the Commissioner had a few days after my arrival at my request made over to me a large extent of river-frontage for a timber depôt. In the forests the timber is dragged to the water's edge by Elephants, buffaloes or oxen, and then floated to market.

* 1891.		Square miles.		Population.
Irawadi Division	...	... 17,542	...	... 1,552,000
Pegu ,,	...	... 9,299	...	... 1,456,000
Toungoo district	...	... 6,354	...	... 162,000
	Total	... 33,195	...	... 3,170,000

Teak however does not float, unless it is perfectly dry, and from time immemorial this has been effected by girdling, that is by making a broad circular cut through bark and sap wood into the dark brown heart wood. Within two or three days the leaves wither and the tree dies. Timber thus girdled dries completely and seasons evenly, for it is on all sides freely exposed to sun and wind. Two or three years before felling therefore, Teak trees are girdled.

Fortunately large quantities of dry timber had been left in the forests, partly felled, partly girdled. Notice had previously been given to all those who had formerly worked the forests, to remove their timber. When the time fixed by that notice had expired, I was able to commence operations and to give profitable employment to the people inhabiting the forests and living in their vicinity. By dealing with these people, the Karens and Burmans, direct and not through middlemen, I gained their confidence and goodwill. At a later date I was in a position, to enable those, who by skill and energy had gained my confidence, to purchase Elephants with funds which I advanced them, and thus to bring out heavy timber, which on the hills of Pegu they were unable to manage with their oxen and buffaloes.

It was necessary to produce more revenue, than the old timber left in the forests, which was mostly small and of inferior value, could be expected to yield. Before however girdling operations could be commenced, a working plan had to be prepared, in order to ensure a permanently sustained yield from the forests.

In those days Teak was the only marketable timber, and unfortunately the Teak in Burma does not form pure forests, but grows scattered among Bamboos and other trees, forming less than one tenth of the entire growing stock. At first sight it seemed an impossible task, to work a forest of that description so as to ensure a sustained yield. Each Teak tree cut would make room for valueless trees of other kinds, while less seed would be shed and consequently fewer

Teak seedlings would spring up. I set to work at once, made a rapid exploration of as many forest districts as possible and upon the data collected based a preliminary working plan, under which the trees to be girdled were to be selected during the first 6 years. The Pegu forests were divided into six divisions, one division being taken in hand annually. The main point aimed at was, to girdle sparingly and to select the trees to be girdled with care. This required constant personal supervision and the consequence was, that I was absent from headquarters the greater part of the year. In those days Major (now Major-General) Edward H. Power rendered a service to forest business in Pegu, which has never been sufficiently recognized. Power was Deputy Judge Advocate General at Rangoon, we were great friends, he saw my difficulties, for timber was coming in steadily, the Contractors had to be paid, and the monthly auction sales at the Government timber depot had to be watched. Large sums of money had to be received and paid out, and in those days I had no assistant at headquarters, whom I could sufficiently trust with these large and steadily growing transactions. He offered to help me, and though his hands were full with important military matters, yet he managed, during several seasons, to superintend the business at headquarters, and to keep money matters straight. Simultaneously with the girdling operations a more detailed examination of the forests was made. Based upon the data thus obtained, the preliminary plan was revised from time to time, until, at a much later date, demarcation and organization had sufficiently advanced, to make it possible to prepare detailed working plans for the different forest districts.

Pegu Forests thrown open to Private Enterprise.

In 1858 the forests in the adjoining provinces of Martaban and Tenasserim had been added to my charge. In 1859 the heavy outlay which at first was unavoidable, had been more than covered by the income of that year, and a steadily increasing surplus seemed certain, when circumstances arose, which for a time threatened to put a stop to the development of the system commenced. Rangoon in those days derived its importance mainly from the export of Teak timber, and the ship-building trade carried on by means of the Teak timber brought from the forests. The export of rice, which since that time has given Rangoon a much greater importance, had hardly begun. The merchants of Rangoon naturally desired their business to increase rapidly, and as soon as they realized, that the system introduced by me in 1856 would limit the quantity of timber brought to market, they commenced a vigorous opposition against it. Personally I made a point of keeping on good terms with them, and they tried hard to induce me to allow them to enter the forests and to cut the whole of the mature trees at once. With much eloquence they contended, that ships built of Teak would soon be a thing of the past, that iron would, in shipbuilding as well as for all other purposes, replace the use of wood. The demand for Teak would diminish, prices would fall and in the end Teak would be a drug in the market, and the Teak forests would be valueless.

At that time the Sepoy mutiny of 1857 had saddled the Government of India with an enormous debt. Under these circumstances the merchants of Rangoon urged me to take advantage of the high market rates for Teak then ruling, to realize large sums by the sale to them of all mature timber standing in the forests, and thus immediately to make for Government a large revenue from the forests. A business transacted on so large a scale, they added, would give a great impulse to the prosperity of Rangoon. They appealed to my sense of duty toward the Government which I was serving, to my ambition and to my common sense, and they pictured in the darkest colours the mischief of a Government monopoly and the disastrous consequences of a refusal to back their proposals.

When my friends found that I remained firm, and that

Major Phayre, the Commissioner, refused to yield to their representations, they went to Calcutta, and backed by the influence of the large and powerful mercantile firms, they succeeded. The Government of India ordered the Commissioner to throw open the Pegu Forests to private enterprise, and these orders were sent to Rangoon in February 1861.

These orders had to be carried out, and the result has been very mischievous. Fortunately however, we were not required to throw open the whole of the Forests at once. By that time I had, by means of linear valuation surveys and height measurements, in all forest districts, been able to classify them according to their value. A large area of the less valuable forests were at once let out on 12 years' leases, with the permission to girdle, in other districts permits were given, in some cases for 3, in others for 6 years, under which the permit holder, on payment of certain rates, became the proprietor of the timber extracted by him, being however limited in his operations to the trees girdled by the forest officers. A limited area of the most valuable forests however was for a time retained under the control of the Forest Department.

Without the cordial and unfailing support which Major Phayre gave to my proposals, the damage done to the public interests of the country would have been much greater than it actually was.

Change of Policy.

In November 1861 the measures taken by the Government of India for opening the forests to private enterprise, were reported to the Home Government. Her Majesty's Secretary of State for India strongly disapproved of these measures. His despatch, dated 24th March 1862, is the first document in the Returns on East India Forest Conservancy, ordered by the House of Commons to be printed in August 1871.

The result was, that no more forests were thrown open, and that those which had been leased out were resumed when the leases expired. Some of these contracts had to be cancelled sooner, because it was discovered that the agents of the permit holder had illicitly girdled Teak on a very large scale.

The experience gained here and in the Attaran forests has taught a lesson, which public men in India have gradually learnt. It is not safe in India at present to entrust the management of public forests to private enterprise, the State therefore must step in and undertake the management of this source of public wealth. At first sight this conclusion seems to be at variance with what has here been stated regarding the good management of private forests upon the continent of Europe. Nay, in regard to Great Britain also, the advice has here been given specially *to private proprietors*, to improve the management of their woodlands. The fact is, on the continent of Europe the State has long ago done its duty to the public in this respect. The good management of the State forests has set the example, which private proprietors have followed.

This, it may justly be said, ought also to have been done in Great Britain. The Crown forests ought long ere this to have been placed under good management, in order to show the way to private landowners. The difficulties, it is true, are considerable. The area of the Crown forests is small, and most of them are heavily burdened with prescriptive rights, which stand in the way of regular management. Nevertheless, much might be done. Real progress however seems impossible, as long as the appointment of Commissioner of Woods and Forests is given, not to a professional forester, but as is commonly supposed, as a reward for services rendered to the political party in power. That office, as well as the appointments of Deputy Surveyor in the different forests, ought long ere this to have been given to experienced foresters. The majority of Indian forest officers have received a thorough professional training, many of them have done eminent service in India, the experience gained in that country would enable them to do exactly what is wanted for the Crown forests of England. The career of an Indian officer as a rule is cut short on his attaining the age of 55, and many would be glad to retire at an earlier age, if they saw a chance of employment in their profession at home. The number of good men available is large, Her Majesty's Government would have the choice, if they could be induced to insist upon a good management of the Crown forests, so as to set an example to private proprietors.

In India there is a special difficulty. Private enterprise at present means European private enterprise, and Europeans in business in India as a rule have one aim only, that is, to get rich as quickly as possible. It is not impossible that in course of time the development of Tea and Coffee plantations will bring about a change in that respect, that is, people will gradually lay greater stress upon maintaining and improving the productiveness, the capital value of their estates, than upon high dividends. Native forest proprietors in several provinces have already commenced to imitate the example set them by the British Government in forest management. What is ordinarily understood as European private enterprise in India however, has not yet attained to that point.

With the interruption caused by the orders of Government in 1861, to throw open the forests to private enterprise, the forests continued to be worked upon the system initiated in 1856. In 1861 the whole of the coast provinces of Burma were united and placed under one Chief Commissioner, Colonel Phayre, the following remarks therefore will relate to the whole of the forests of this province, with the exception of Arakan, which has no forests producing Teak. An important feature in the system initiated in 1856 was the care of the Teak trees and particularly of the self sown seedlings, which fortunately were found to be abundant in the forests. Whenever girdling operations were undertaken in any forest district, and also on other occasions, when work was going on, Teak trees were cleared of creepers, other trees overshadowing young Teak were cut, and all heavy inflammable matter, wood, branches, dry brushwood, in the vicinity of seedlings was cleared away. These operations were very beneficial, but it was clear to me from the outset that something more was wanted, that it was not sufficient to protect and aid the Teak which had sprung up naturally, but that it would be necessary to increase the proportion of Teak in the forests by sowing and planting. The small experimental plantations formed in 1856 and 1857 were successful, the difficulty however was, in the forest, where the tree grows best, always to command the needful labour at moderate cost.

Plantations:

The inhabitants of these forests, Karens and in some places Burmans, raise their crops, rice, cotton, vegetables, by means of a rude system of shifting cultivation. In the dry season the forest is cut. When dry the tangled mass of Bamboos and branches is fired, and after the first showers in May the paddy is sown in shallow holes made with a narrow spade. The crops are reaped during the ensuing dry season. In the following year another piece of forest is taken in hand, and so on, until after the lapse of say 20 to 30 years, the forest on the first piece has grown up sufficiently to admit of again being cut, burnt and sown. These hill clearings in Burma are known as Toungyas. A similar practice exists, as previously stated, under the name of Kumri in Madras and under other names in other provinces. As soon as I had seen the first Karen Toungya in 1856, I determined to devise some method, by which this mode of shifting cultivation might be utilized for planting Teak on a large scale in the forests. A few small experimental plots were actually thus planted in 1856 and succeeding years, by a Burmese forester in the Kaboung forests. Upon a large scale however Toungya Teak plantations were not established until many years later. It was Major (now Major-General) Seaton, an officer in one of the Madras regiments, at that time stationed at Rangoon, whom I had, together with other military officers, engaged for service in the forests. He gradually rose to be Conservator, and having succeeded in gaining the confidence of the Karens in several forest districts, he induced them to plant Teak with paddy upon their hill clearings, certain rates being paid for each acre with the stipulated number of plants one year old. The first Toungya Teak plantations on a large scale were made in 1868, and since then the system has developed well. In 1880 an aggregate area of 2,515 acres had thus been planted, at a total cost of 24,932 Rupees, or less than 10 Rupees an acre. In 1895 the area had been increased to 35,551 acres. Other plantations by means of hired labour were made in some of the easier accessible forest districts and on the outskirts of the forests, and here also field crops were raised with the Teak. In 1895 the area of these plantations aggregated 4,001 acres.

It has been explained above that Teak is most commonly found scattered in Bamboo forests. In Burma many species of Bamboo are associated with Teak and most of these come into flower periodically. When this takes place, all stems of one bush cover themselves with flowers in the place of leaves, and all bushes in one district generally flower simultaneously. After the seed has ripened, the stems die and the dry stems are gradually consumed by the jungle fires of the hot season. At that time therefore the cover overhead in the forest is suddenly removed and the seedlings of Teak and other trees get a chance to grow up. Obviously this opportunity may be used to plant Teak on a large scale in these clearances. Berthold Ribbentrop, the present Inspector-General of Forests in India, has the great merit of having been the first to employ this system on a large scale. In 1895 3,744 acres had been stocked with Teak in places where the Bamboo had flowered.

The different species behave differently in this respect and hitherto operations have been confined to localities stocked with Dendrocalamus strictus, a species which flowers frequently on limited areas. Some foresters in Burma hold, that when operations are commenced in areas stocked with those species which flower simultaneously over large areas, such as Bambusa polymorpha, Teak may be planted on so large a scale that Toungya and other plantations may then be given up.

Altogether in 1895 an area aggregating 43,296 acres had been planted, chiefly with Teak, in lower Burma, and this area is being extended steadily. This alone will assure a considerable annual yield of Teak timber. The most recent researches regarding Teak grown in Pegu under the regime of the annual jungle fires, have established the age of a tree 6 ft. in girth to be between 134 and 156 years. In plantations, however, from which fire is kept out, the growth is much more rapid, and we are justified in assuming, that in such places 90 years will suffice to bring up a tree to that size. The area artificially stocked with Teak in 1895 may be expected to furnish permanently an annual yield of 1,250,000 cub. ft. In the six years ending with 1894-95 on an average 3,281,000 cub. ft. of Teak timber were extracted from the forests of lower Burma. Hence more than one-third of the present annual yield furnished by the natural forests has already been assured by means of the plantations. This satisfactory result is entirely due to the excellent Officers who since 1868 have successively held the post of Conservator of Forests in lower Burma, and it seems right to mention here specially, besides Major Seaton, Mr. Ribbentrop and Mr. H. C. Hill.

Demarcation of Forests. Karen areas.

In a country so thinly inhabited, as Pegu and the adjoining province of Tenasserim were in those days, considerable progress could be made in forest business without setting apart and demarcating those forest tracts that are to be permanently maintained as State Forests. Vigorous action in this matter was not commenced until 1876, twenty years after the first preliminary working plan of the forests had been prepared. The main difficulty consisted in the shifting Toungya cultivation. It has above been explained, that in 1848 Kumri cultivation was stopped in Mysore and that in 1860 the practice was prohibited, special cases excepted, in the Government forests of the Madras Presidency, but that in both territories these orders were subsequently relaxed. In Burma no such thing was ever attempted. Karens, and in some places Burmans, had from time immemorial lived upon the produce of their toungyas, subject only, under Burmese and English rule, to the prohibition of cutting the Royal Teak tree. Fortunately the area of forest at the disposal of Government was large and thus it was possible to assign to each village, that had hitherto practised Toungya cultivation in the forests, an area sufficient for their requirements in this respect, in which they were at liberty, without let or hindrance, to carry on their clearings, allowing for a certain increase of population. In 1895 the demarcated reserved forests in lower Burma aggregated 4,525,000 acres, and in this area were included a large number of Karen areas, aggregating 364,000 acres. This destructive mode of cultivation is now confined within definite limits. And there is another advantage. The Karens are gradually abandoning their nomadic habits, they establish permanent paddy fields in the valleys and by terracing the hills, they plant gardens and groves of fruit trees. The money which they have earned by timber work and by planting Teak, enables them to purchase cattle, and they thus gradually rise in the scale of civilization. The introduction of systematic forestry has been beneficial to these rude forest tribes.

Yield of Forests.

The yield of the lower Burma Forests in timber as well as in money has increased gradually and steadily, and there is good ground for anticipating that this increase will be maintained.

Periods.	Teak timber extracted annually. Cubic feet.	Annual net revenue. Rupees.
12 years, 1856-57 to 1867-68	1,260,000	208,000
6 years, 1889-90 to 1894-95	3,281,000	1,865,000

Thus, while the Anamalay and other Teak forests of the Madras Presidency, previously mentioned, were overworked when forest management commenced, so that little mature and sound Teak now remains, the annual yield in Teak timber of the lower Burma forests has nearly trebled, since work was commenced on a regular system. So much for the value of a working plan, however rough at the outset, and however incomplete the data upon which it originally was based.

To some extent the increased outturn of timber has been due to the circumstance, that large areas of Teak-producing forest had formerly been closed against the extraction of timber by obstructions in the rivers. Some of these obstructions were caused by the silting up of mountain streams coming down during the rains with great velocity, carrying with them masses of sand, silt and rubbish, which they deposited on entering the level country of the main valley. The other class was caused by boulders and barriers of rock in the bed of the hill streams. The removal of these obstructions by blasting rocks, digging canals, and other works was begun in 1858. These works are still progressing, they have opened up a large area of valuable forest, from which formerly it was impossible to bring out the timber.

Besides the Teak timber here stated, of late years timber of other kinds also, as well as bamboos, has been extracted, and has contributed a small portion of the revenue. Teak timber however still remains the most important product of these forests.

The management of the Burma Forests has done good so far, as it has established two important facts :

(1) Indian forests can be so managed as to give a permanent and annually increasing yield in timber and money, while their productiveness and their capital value is increased.

(2) These results it is possible to obtain, while promoting the welfare, and securing the good will of the people living within and in the vicinity of the forests.

The system initiated in the coast provinces, was, on the annexation of upper Burma in 1886, introduced in that territory, and the results have been equally satisfactory. The mean annual net revenue of upper and lower Burma during the 6 years from 1889/90 to 1894/95 has been as follows:

	Rupees.
Lower Burma	1,865,000
Upper ,,	1,443,000
	3,308,000

The success of forest administration in upper Burma is due to two distinguished Conservators, fortunately still in the service, H. C. Hill, already mentioned, who had received his professional training in France, and J. W. Oliver, who had learnt in Germany under the late Forst-director Burckhardt. During the same period the annual net revenue of the Government forests in all provinces of the British Indian Empire, including the Presidencies of Madras and Bombay, has amounted to 7,357,000 Rupees. Thus the net forest revenue of Burma amounts to forty-five per cent. of that produced by the forests of the entire British Indian Empire. The forest policy in Burma was laid down by Lord Dalhousie. His far-sighted admonition at the outset, was invaluable in so far, as it gave confidence, that the mistaken measures subsequently adopted by Government would not prevail, but would in the end give way to a sound forest policy. Without that confidence the whole undertaking would most probably have come to nothing.

Forest Administration in other Provinces.

I must now ask the reader to go back to 1861. In November of that year Dr. Cleghorn was directed to proceed from Madras to the Punjab, in order to examine the forests of the North Western Himalaya, as well as the brushwood tracts of the plains. The exploration of the forests in the hills occupied the summer months of 1862 and 1863, while the winter months were devoted to the inspection of timber depots and Rakhs in the plains. His Report, which was published in 1864, has been of great value in furnishing the data, whereupon soon afterwards forest administration in the Punjab was based. This important measure was taken in the Public Works Department of the Government of India, the Secretary in that Department being the late Sir Henry Yule. The orders for throwing open the Pegu Forests to private enterprise, which it will be remembered were issued in February 1861, were passed in the Foreign Department, to which at that time the entire administration of Pegu was subordinate, while the civil administration in the older provinces was under the Home Department. Soon after those orders had been passed, the subject had been reconsidered by the Government of India. Doubts were entertained, whether it had been right, to deviate from the policy laid down in regard to the Pegu Forests by Lord Dalhousie, and it was decided in future to deal with questions of forest administration in all provinces of the Empire in one Department. As the Secretary in the Public Works Department (Colonel Yule) and his Successor, Colonel (now Lieutenant-General) Richard Strachey, took a special interest in forest conservancy, that Department was chosen, and one of the first measures taken was the deputation of Dr. Cleghorn to the Punjab.

In a despatch to the Secretary of State for India, dated 1st November 1862, the Government of India said: "The serious question presents itself for consideration, how we may best secure the development of some real system of forest administration, for at present it is certain, that nothing deserving the name exists. And the necessity of placing the forest business upon a definite footing, and of arranging that all matters connected with it shall be dealt with in one Department, seems obvious."* At the same time the writer of these lines was summoned to Calcutta, to advise the Government of India as well as local Governments in the matter of organizing their forest business. Subsequently, in 1864 he was appointed Inspector-General of Forests. It would be beyond the scope of the present publication, to give a comprehensive account of the further progress of forest business; it must suffice to touch upon a few points of special importance.

Protection of Forests against Fire.

I began my work in the Central Provinces, where Mr. (now Right Honble. Sir Richard) Temple was the Chief Commissioner. In December 1860, Mr. Temple had been sent to Burma on a special mission. He was present at a large meeting of timber merchants, which the Commissioner had convened to discuss with me the then burning question of opening the forests to private enterprise, and I had afterwards the privilege of conducting him over the large timber depot on the Salween river above Maulmein. Afterwards, when he fully appreciated the important interests at stake, he became a staunch friend of progress in forestry, he had appointed an excellent officer as Conservator of Forests in the Central Provinces, Major (now Colonel) G. F. Pearson, and he gave to all my proposals regarding the forests of those provinces his powerful support. My chief aim in that part of the country was, to make an attempt to protect the forests against the ravages of the fires of the hot season. Excepting the Himalaya, the most valuable forests in most provinces consist of trees which are leafless during part of the dry season.

* Parliamentary Return on Forest Conservancy, Part I., India, p. 7.

In these forests leaves, twigs, herbs and grass, everything becomes as dry as tinder during the hot season, the smallest spark is sufficient to set this dry material on fire, and these fires spread over the whole country. In forests and grass lands these fires have from time immemorial been a regular institution. Fires devastate in the same way the Pine forests in the Himalaya and on the mountains of Assam and Burma. Dense evergreen forests, which cover large areas in the moister regions of India, are not as a rule invaded by these fires, and there are limited tracts of deciduous forests in moist localities, which escape in favourable seasons. To these annually recurring fires was chiefly due the poor condition in which a large portion of the Indian forests was found, when regular management was commenced. In Burma the position of forest conservancy had been too uncertain, to attempt so difficult a task as fire protection, moreover the difficulties were much greater than in the drier climate and less luxuriant vegetation of the Central Provinces. But to interfere with this ancient institution, which cleared the ground in the hot season of inconvenient grass and underwood, seemed little short of impious interference with time-hallowed custom. Major Pearson himself had serious doubts on the subject, he knew that the measure would be distasteful to all, Europeans as well as natives. Nevertheless he determined to make the attempt, he selected the Bori forest, a district most favourably situated for the experiment, as it was protected on the west side by a river 50 to 100 yards wide, while on the north the steep sandstone scarp of the Pachmarhi hills, made the inroad of fire from that side impossible. This work he commenced in the dry season of 1865. He succeeded, and within a few years he saw the condition of the forest entirely altered. The blanks were filling up with self-sown seedlings, into the extensive grass lands the growth of trees extended steadily from the edge of the forest, the trees increased rapidly in height and girth, and the fresh shoots of the Bamboo became taller and stouter. The great and unexpected success in this place encouraged him to extend his operations, and to him is due the credit of having, in the teeth of powerful opposition, proved that the exclusion of the annual fires is possible, and that it is beneficial. His successor Captain (now Colonel) Doveton steadily extended the work in a methodical manner, he brought down the expense of these operations to a minimum, and it is much to be regretted, that a year ago the 55 years rule has compelled his retirement. From the Central Provinces Colonel Pearson was transferred to the more important charge of the North-West Provinces, and there also he succeeded in establishing an effective system of fire protection. Of the $47\frac{1}{2}$ million acres of Reserved forests in the British Indian Empire, including forests leased from native states, no less than 17 million acres, or 36 % were successfully protected from fire in 1895.

Organization of Establishments.

In the organization of forest establishments the leading principle followed was decentralization. The management of the business in each province was left entirely to the Government of that province, the Government of India reserving to itself the right of insisting upon the maintenance of correct principles. The chief Forest officer in each province was styled Conservator of forests, and in subordination to the local Government, this officer had the control of the entire forest business in that province. At a later period decentralization has been extended downwards. In those districts, where forests existed, the officers in charge of Forest divisions were placed in subordination to the chief civil officer of that district, the Collector or Deputy Commissioner. At the outset this would have been impossible. Systematic forestry was a subject entirely foreign to the majority of civil officers, and the only plan to ensure vigorous action in the right direction, was to appoint one chief forest officer in each province, who would, subject to the control of the Local

Government, take the initiative, and organize the protection, improvement and working of the forests. Take for instance the protection of forests against fire. Many, perhaps most civil officers at that time were utterly hostile to this interference with old established custom, they regarded the measures proposed as Utopian, as the outcome of theoretical speculations. A new Department therefore had to be formed in each province, and this raised grave doubts in the minds of many thoughtful public officers.

In January 1864 Sir John (afterwards Lord) Lawrence landed in Calcutta as Governor-General of India. By strong, just and considerate patriarchal government, Lawrence had so attached the people of the Punjab to British rule, as to enable him to save the British Indian Empire during the Mutiny of 1857, mainly through the resources of that province and the fidelity of its people. This result he had attained by insisting upon personal government by his district Officers. The chief civil officer he held must be supreme in his district, and there must be no departmental interference of any sort. When Lawrence came home in 1859, he took his place as a Member of the Council of India. He saw the despatches sent home in the matter of forest administration, and he did not approve of the plan to establish a new Department, that would have charge of the waste and forest lands, and that might in many cases interfere with the supreme authority of the chief civil officer in his district.

Lawrence had summoned some of his old Punjab Officers to meet him on arrival at Calcutta, and it is no secret, that he expressed to them his determination to stamp out this new fangled scheme. Lawrence was essentially a strong man, who would carry out what he had determined upon, regardless of personal considerations. But Richard Strachey, then Secretary in the Public Works Department, was in charge of the forest business. He was equal to the occasion, he succeeded in preventing precipitate action, and gradually induced Lawrence to see, that some organization of forest business was absolutely necessary for the welfare of the country. Sir John Lawrence soon learnt to value Colonel Strachey's powerful help in extending irrigation works on a large scale, and later on in devising a system of Railways to be built by the State. It was due to Richard Strachey's steadily growing influence, and to the patient perseverance and excellent tact of his successor Colonel Dickens, that Lawrence as Governor-General sanctioned a definite organization of the new Department in all provinces. I had the great satisfaction of learning in Summer 1868, the last season he spent at Simla, from Sir John Lawrence himself, that he was pleased with the organization of forest business.

Constant attacks of Jungle fever, which had commenced in 1859 in Burma, had gradually weakened my constitution and necessitated furlough. While in Europe, in 1866, I succeeded in obtaining permission to engage for the Government of India two capable young forest officers from Germany. Dr. William Schlich, the author of the excellent work mentioned at the outset, now at the head of the Cooper's Hill Forest School, who succeeded me as Inspector-General of Forests, when I left India in 1883, was enlisted by me in Hesse-Darmstadt, where he was regarded as the most promising among the men of his standing. Mr. Berthold Ribbentrop, the present Inspector-General of Forests in India, came from Hanover, where he had worked under Forst-director Burckhardt, one of the most eminent foresters in Germany.

I further was permitted, while in Europe, to organize a system of selecting annually a number of young Englishmen for forest service in India, and of giving them a professional training, practical and theoretical, in the State Forests of France and Prussia. My plans for the professional training of Candidates for the Indian Forest Service attracted the attention of Sir James Fergusson, then Under Secretary of State, and through him I obtained the powerful support of the present Marquis of Salisbury, then, as Lord Cranborne, Secretary of State for India. The first batch of men, who had received their professional education in this manner, arrived in India, December 1869, and the system was continued, until in 1885 a Forest school was established in England by Dr. Schlich, in connection with the Royal Engineering College at Cooper's Hill. For the men thus sent out annually, it became necessary, to provide definite prospects of advancement, and this led to the organization of the superior or controlling forest service, which was proposed by the Government of India in September, and sanctioned by Her Majesty's Secretary of State in November 1868. Under the Conservator in each province, a graded list of Deputy and Assistant Conservators was provided, who should henceforth as a rule be recruited from England. The necessity was now recognized of employing specially trained officers in the administration of the forests, so as "to guard against the ruin of one of the most important sources of national wealth, if the care of the forests were left to ignorant persons."* The Scheme, before being submitted to the Home Government, had been circulated for an expression of opinion to all local Governments, and it is amusing now to read in the Blue Book quoted, the objections raised against it at the time by the local authorities. Sir John Lawrence however remained firm, and it was under his orders that the scheme was finally worked out.

Indian Forest Floras.

The total area of the British Indian Empire is 1,560,000 Square miles, that of Europe aggregates 3,800,000. Yet the number of trees indigenous in India exceeds 1,200, while in Europe only 158 species are known. And besides these trees there are 120 species of Bamboos and a large number of Climbers, which play an important part in the Indian forests, being either useful or injurious. The forester finds himself bewildered by this overwhelming variety of

* Parliamentary Return on Forest Conservancy, Part I., India, 1871, p. 404.

forest vegetation. Few can attempt to acquire a knowledge of all these species, but a large number of the more important kinds the Indian Forester must know, if he is to do his work. In each country of Europe, where regular forest administration has been established, handbooks of the trees and shrubs of the forest have been published for the special use of foresters, indeed in Germany alone a considerable number of such handbooks exists. Even in the United States of North America, where no regular forest administration has been attempted by the State, and where small beginnings only have been made by private proprietors, a large work, of which ten quarto volumes already have appeared, will shortly be completed, in wise anticipation of the necessity that will arise when forest administration is attempted on a large scale.* In India the want of such books made itself felt at an early date. Colonel Beddome, who succeeded Dr. Cleghorn as Conservator of Forests in Madras, was the first in the field. His Flora Sylvatica of Southern India and Ceylon appeared 1869 to 1873 in three quarto volumes with a large number of good illustrations. In 1874 was published the Forest Flora of North-West and Central India, which had been commenced by the late Dr. Stewart, the first Conservator of Forests in the Punjab, and completed by the writer of these lines. In 1878 Sulpiz Kurz, the Curator of the Herbarium at the Royal Botanic Gardens, Calcutta, whose premature death was a great loss for forest Botany, published a Forest Flora for lower Burma in two volumes. Mr. James Sykes Gamble, formerly Conservator of Forests in Bengal, and now Director of the Dehra Dún Forest School and Conservator of the School Forests, in 1877 published a List of trees, shrubs and large Climbers of the Darjiling district and a new edition of this useful little work appeared in 1896. The same author published in 1881 a Manual of Indian timbers, and in 1896 a splendid work with excellent

* The Silva of North America. By Charles Sprague Sargent, Boston and New York.

illustrations of the Indian Bamboos. Lastly Mr. W. A. Talbot, Deputy Conservator of Forests in the Bombay Presidency, in 1894 brought out a most useful work upon the trees of that part of the country.

It is here the place to mention the "Indian Forester," a Magazine of Forestry, started as a quarterly, and continued as a monthly publication, which was commenced by Dr. Schlich in 1875 and subsequently continued by the Officers who have successively held the post of Director of the Forest School. This periodical, of which 22 volumes have appeared, contains a large variety of valuable papers upon Indian Forestry. In other respects also, Indian Foresters have contributed their share to the development of a literature on forest matters in the English language.

Forest Legislation.

As a tentative measure a Forest Act (VII. of 1865) was passed in Sir John Lawrence's time. This Act however was imperfect, and as early as 1869 attempts were made to amend it. As far as I had something to do with this, I had the advice and assistance of my old friend Sir William Markby, at that time Judge of the High Court, Calcutta, and of Mr. B. H. Baden-Powell, the author of the lectures on Forest Law previously mentioned, and afterwards Judge of the Chief Court of the Punjab. However, my business merely was to submit proposals, the Acts were drafted and passed in the Legislative Council, and the result was not always in accordance with the proposals which I had submitted. Forest legislation is an intricate business in all countries, and in India it is particularly difficult. On the present occasion it would be quite impossible to enter into it, and it must suffice to draw attention to the fundamental question, the rights of the State and of other persons in the forests.

The British Government has legally succeeded to the rights actually exercised by the former rulers of conquered or ceded States, at the time of conquest or cession. But the intention of the British Government has always been, to use these rights, in order to promote the welfare of the people in those territories. It is not here the place to explain, how occupied and cultivated lands have been dealt with ; the unoccupied waste, including forests, as a rule was the property of the State. This proprietary right in waste and forest, however, had in many cases been deliberately alienated. Instances are the Zemindari estates created in Bengal under the permanent settlement of 1793, the Talukdárs of Oudh, the Malguzars in some districts of the Central Provinces, the village estates of Ajmere-Merwara, as well as the lands sold or leased under the waste land rules. Those waste or forest lands, in which the proprietary right of Government had not been alienated, or where older proprietary rights had not been expressly recognized, as for instance in Malabar, were at the disposal of Government, and upon this is based the provision in the Indian Forest Laws, which authorizes Government to constitute such lands reserved or State Forests.

In these waste and forest lands, however, the people living on these lands or in their vicinity, had grazed their cattle, had cut wood and bamboos for their use and had cleared land for shifting or permanent cultivation. This customary user of the forest was, it is true, exercised under the old native Governments, subject to the pleasure of the ruling power. Native Rulers in many cases restricted or extinguished this customary user of forest and waste lands. Hence it was not plain at the outset, how the Law should deal with these customs. My deliberate opinion from the beginning was, as has already been stated, that this customary user must be regarded as a right, that the growth of forest rights in India had been analogous to the growth of similar rights of user in Europe.* In a paper, which

* Brandis, Memorandum on forest legislation proposed for British India, p. 13.—Simla, 1875.

I read at the Meeting of the British Association, Brighton, 1872,* I said:

"There has been much thoughtless talk, as if the natives of India, in burning the forests and destroying them by their erratic clearings, were committing some grave offence. If the matter is carefully analysed, they will be found to have the same sort of prescription, which justifies the Commoner in the New Forest to exercise his right of pasture, mast and turbary. Such rights, when the public benefit requires it, must be extinguished; but the wild tribes of India have the same claim as the holder of prescriptive forest rights in Europe, to demand that provision be made for their reasonable wants and requirements."

This view of the case was accepted, the waste and forest lands therefore were held to be not necessarily at the absolute disposal of Government, but often as burdened with prescriptive rights of other persons. On the other hand I maintained, that Government, as the guardian of all public interests, must insist upon the regulation of these rights, so as to render possible a good management of the reserved forests in the interests of the country generally. I further maintained, that Government must be at liberty to extinguish these rights in any particular forest area, liberal compensation being given for the loss of these rights in the shape of money payment or the grant of land. Hence, when it was decided, to constitute any waste or Forest land a reserved or State forest, it was necessary to invite claimants to come forward in order to prove their rights. The duty of deciding, which claims might be admitted as a right, as well as the regulation and commutation of rights thus admitted, is under the Indian Forest Laws entrusted to special Officers, the forest settlement officers. An appeal from the decisions of these Officers is provided. The Indian Forest Laws, like those of Europe, contain another provision of great im-

* Reprinted from Ocean Highways, October, 1872, in Transactions of the Scotch Arboricultural Society, Vol. VII., p. 113.

portance, viz., that in land duly declared a reserved forest no right can be acquired by prescription.

Upon these principles have been based three principal Forest Laws: The Indian Forest Act of 1878, the Burma Forest Act of 1881 and the Madras Forest Act of 1882. For some districts and provinces, where the Governor General in Council has power to make rules having the force of Law, such as Berar, Hazara, Ajmere, Upper Burma, special Forest Regulations were passed. Under these Acts and Regulations penalties are prescribed for offences committed against the Forest Law and it is a noteworthy fact, that offences punished under the Forest laws have upon the whole not been numerous. This may be taken as a proof that the changes, which the efficient protection and the regular management of the forests have necessarily introduced into the habits of the people in and near the forests, have been made gradually, and as a rule with due regard to their feelings.

Tanning Materials, Caoutchouc, Iron.

Timber, wood and bamboos form what may be termed the principal produce of forests. There are however other products besides these. Bark and leaves of many trees are used for tanning. Myrobalans, the fruit of Terminalia Chebula, is employed for the same purpose, and is exported from Bombay on a considerable scale. Of these substances a permanent and sufficient supply has been ensured by the measures taken for the establishment, protection and good management of public forests in the different provinces. The same may be said regarding the supply of Cutch, the extract of the heartwood of Acacia Catechu, at least as far as Burma is concerned. Formerly the trees used to be cut wholesale in order to prepare this substance, and at one time the exhaustion of this valuable produce seemed imminent. Since 1876 however large areas of forest, producing this tree, have been constituted State Forests, plantations of Acacia Catechu have been made and no apprehensions on this account need now be entertained.

A most important product is India Rubber, the milky juice of Ficus elastica. This tree grows north of 24° N. Lat., scattered in the moist forests of Assam, East Bengal and upper Burma. Since these countries have been opened by River steamers, roads and railways, Caoutchouc has become an important article of export from Calcutta and Rangoon. Formerly the trees were tapped wherever found, and the result has been wholesale destruction. In the richest parts not more than 10 to 20 Rubber trees on the square mile exist, and when a commencement was made to form State forests in Assam, very few of these trees were left. Nearly the whole of the rubber exported at present, is brought from forests situated beyond the frontier, or from districts, where forest operations have not yet been commenced. Under these circumstances there was no alternative. If it was intended to secure a permanent yield of this article in future, it was necessary to plant the tree upon a large scale.

Mr. Gustav Mann at that time was Chief Forest Officer in Assam, and it is due to his skill and energy, that between 1875 and 1884 upwards of 900 acres were planted up. In 1884 the Chief Commissioner of the province recommended, that the plantations should not be extended, and that the further development of this industry should be left to private enterprise. The magnificent development of the tea plantations in Assam, after Government had set the example by establishing the first garden in 1835, had shown, what can be accomplished by private enterprise in this direction. Nevertheless, there is a great difference. A tea plantation yields an annual return, a few years after it has been formed, while an India Rubber tree must be 50 years old, before it can be tapped.* Very properly therefore the Government of India at that time declined to

* The Mexican Caoutchouc tree (Castilloa elastica) yields a return when 8 years old. Accordingly large plantations have been established, for the purchase and working of which, a Joint Stock Company has lately been formed. Apart from the planted forests of Casuarina on the Coromandel coast near Madras, the only instance of plantations made by private enterprise in the East, of trees which yield no return, until they

accept the Chief Commissioner's recommendation. Operations were continued until 1893, when an aggregate area of 2100 acres had been planted. However, in 1894 the Government of India decided to stop further extension, because doubts were entertained, whether the expenditure would prove remunerative, and further because, even if it were remunerative, many years must elapse, before any profits could be obtained.

And yet it is well known, that the natural resources of Caoutchouc all over the world are gradually getting exhausted, while the article is indispensable for electrical and many other industries. India Rubber has justly been designated as one of the prime necessities of civilization. The demand is increasing, while the supply is diminishing, consequently prices are rising and may be expected to rise further. The annual rubber export from Assam is worth in Calcutta 350,000 Rupees, and the Government royalty on this quantity amounts to 42,000 Rupees a year. This revenue is derived from the extermination of the natural rubber trees, it will diminish and will finally cease altogether. It would seem to be in accordance with common sense, to spend a portion of this income upon extending the plantations, and thus eventually to realize a certain and steadily increasing revenue, and, what is more important, to ensure a permanent and increasing export from Calcutta of an indispensable article.

In many other directions forests might and should be utilized, to develop the resources of India, to a greater extent than has hitherto been done. The old native iron and steel industry has in many districts almost ceased, and this need not have been the case, had more attention been paid to the subject. Steel and wrought iron of the very best description have from time immemorial been made

---

have attained a great age, is the attempt said to have been made within the last year or two, of planting forests of the Gutta Percha tree in North Borneo on behalf of a company interested in the construction of submarine Telegraphs.

with charcoal in innumerable small furnaces. In order to produce the large quantities of charcoal required, wood formerly was cut in an irregular and wasteful manner, without any regard to the regeneration of the forest. At the same time the growing population required more wood for other purposes, and the result was, that in many places the furnaces could no longer be worked. Where however reserved forests have been formed and have been efficiently protected, the position of matters has become completely altered. It has been explained, that protection against fire has gradually changed the condition of the forests. Where formerly they were open, irregularly and incompletely stocked, they are now dense and compact. In this process of improvement the less valuable kinds have profited equally with those which, like Teak and others, yield valuable timber. Yet most of these less valuable kinds, which as a rule constitute the great mass of the forests, furnish charcoal that can be used in iron making. Soon after the changes in the condition of the forests through strict protection had become manifest, it became evident, that the enormously increased production of the inferior woods threatened to become a real difficulty, unless means were found to utilize them. Iron making naturally suggested itself as likely to help in the employment of these inferior woods, and thus to make room for the more valuable kinds.

In many districts, where mineral coal does not occur, particularly in the southern portion of the peninsula, extensive deposits of excellent iron ore are found, hæmatite in Bellary, and Magnetic iron ore in the Salem district. There is hardly any district in the Madras Presidency and in Mysore, without deposits of iron ore. Between 1824 and 1867 repeated attempts have been made to carry on charcoal iron manufacture on a large scale in the Salem district. These attempts have failed, because no adequate measures were taken to secure a permanent supply of wood to make charcoal. The necessity of having a sufficient area of forest well stocked, efficiently protected and regularly managed, never seems to have been realized by the promoters and Managers of the different Companies that have successively attempted this work. The last year of my Indian Service, from November 1881 to January 1883 I spent in the Madras Presidency, and in my Report upon the Forests I submitted definite proposals regarding what should be done, in the interests of the country, to develop the old Native charcoal Iron industry.* My proposals aimed at two distinct objects. *First* to arrange for the efficient protection and good management of a sufficient area of forest in the vicinity of the old Native Iron works, so as to enable them to continue their operations. *Second* to attach a competent Metallurgist to the Madras Forest Department, in order to start operations on Government account for the improvement of the Native Method.

It would lead too far on the present occasion, were I to enter into detail, and it must suffice to say, that in the opinion of competent experts a substantial improvement of the Native method is feasible. Indian charcoal-iron can never compete with the ordinary kinds of iron and steel which are made with mineral coal. These are now produced in Europe and North America in enormous and steadily increasing quantities and are sold at extremely low prices. Competition with these is out of the question. But Swedish pig iron made with charcoal fetches from 80 to 100 shillings a ton, while English pig made with mineral coal only fetches from 35 to 40 shillings. The object must be, to enable the Native iron smelter, by means of an improved and less wasteful process, to manufacture an article approaching in quality the excellent steel and wrought iron, that was formerly produced on a large scale in Southern India.

No action was taken upon my proposals of 1883 and a paper published in the Indian Forester in 1894 on the same subject has also remained unheeded. If not too late, this is a great opportunity for contributing materially to the

* Brandis, Suggestions regarding Forest Administration in the Madras Presidency. Chapter III. : Forests and Iron—VIII. : Bellary; IX. : Salem.

further development of the resources of India. At the same time, the extended employment of the less valuable woods for iron making, will greatly facilitate the management of many forest districts.

Cattle Fodder.

Other substances without number, necessary for the everyday life of the people, and required for the commerce of the world, might be produced in steadily increasing quantities. But the indispensable condition is efficient protection and good management of a sufficient forest area in the different provinces. In a most forcible manner this is illustrated by a most humble produce of the Indian forest, grass and cattle fodder. It has been mentioned above, that the Native chiefs in Rajputana fully appreciated the fact, that in the dry climate of that country a good crop of grass is produced under the shade of trees, when in the open no grass can live and the ground is bare. And the famine of 1867 to 1869 has taught the lesson, that while the cattle in Kishangarh and Bednore were saved by the fodder furnished by the forest, in the adjoining British territory with its denuded hills, the cattle perished. True, it was difficult to devise a remedy. The State had at settlement relinquished its right over the waste lands. But the people had neglected to fulfil the conditions under which the grant was made.

Colonel Keatinge V.C. who was then Agent to the Governor General in Rajputana, and Commissioner of Ajmere, was strongly impressed with the necessity of taking action and the proposal which I made in 1869, to place the principal ranges of hills, running through the district, under protection, met with his approval. Subsequently, in January 1871, I submitted definite proposals to the Government of India, and again urged action after returning from furlough in 1874. It was the late Sir Charles Aitchison, then Secretary in the Foreign Department, who drafted the Ajmere Forest Regulation, and obtained the consent to it from Lord Northbrook, at that time Viceroy and Governor

General of India. This Forest Regulation gave the Chief Commissioner of Ajmere power to take up any tract of waste or hilly land as a State forest, granting the people, who had formerly an interest in that land, the right of cutting grass and wood in it and a liberal share of the net proceeds from the management of such lands. The proprietary rights, which had been granted at the settlement, were thus annulled, but the measure was framed in as considerate a manner, as was possible under the circumstances of the case. At first sight this seemed to be a confiscation of rights deliberately granted. In reality however the waste lands had been granted to the village communities. They were communal lands, and as such public, not private property. Government therefore, as the guardian of all public interests, had the duty to interfere. Anything like arbitrary action was utterly repugnant to the feelings of my old friend Aitchison, but he saw, the measure was necessary, in order to guard, if possible, against distress and misery in seasons of drought. And this small measure might, if properly followed up, have proved to be one of the most beneficial measures passed in the reign of Lord Northbrook. Action was taken cautiously, and on a visit in December, 1878, I found that 12 tracts aggregating 64,428 acres had been taken up under the Regulation.

The management of these lands was left entirely in the hands of the civil officers, under whom were placed subordinate forest officers. In the commencement a superior forest officer, Mr. McArthur Moir and afterwards Mr. Lowrie, were placed in charge, both however working under the Chief Civil Officer's orders. Mr. McArthur Moir and his successors established an effective system of fire protection, where necessary they fenced in the areas by stone walls or hedges of the fleshy Euphorbia. Dams across watercourses were thrown up and plantations were made in suitable places. On my visit in 1878 I found a great and most satisfactory improvement. In many places young forest had grown up, and grass was everywhere abundant. Since then however very little progress has been made, for in 1895 the area had only been increased to 89,178 acres.

In 1892 another regulation was passed, authorizing Government to establish Village Reserves under conditions somewhat differing from those settled in 1874, but only 6,842 acres were taken up under this regulation, so that in 1895 the total area placed under protection amounted to 96,020 acres or 5½ % of the entire area. About one half of the district is in the hands of large land-holders and to the waste and forest included in their estates the regulation does not apply. But had the civil Officers in charge earnestly followed up the good progress made in the commencement, a much larger area might have been taken up, and the benefit to the people would have been real and lasting. More than this. The villagers had been given the right to cut grass in the reserves. The grazing of cattle however had been prohibited, as this would have prevented the improvement of the forest. The plan was, that only in seasons of drought cattle should be admitted. Instead of this, the greater part of the reserves was after a time opened year after year to grazing. In 1890 and 1891 the rains were scanty and the whole of the reserves, with the exception of 1,182 acres, were thrown open to grazing, in accordance with the original plan. But in 1892-93 the rains were unusually good, yet 56·4 % of the area was thrown open; the rains were excellent in 1893-94 and in 1894-95, giving an abundant supply of grass outside the reserves, yet in the first of these two years 58 % and in the last 68 % were thrown open. This action would seem to have been in accordance with the spirit of orders issued a few years ago by the Government of India, "there is a very special benefit to be derived from a relaxation of the restrictions, that have hitherto been too often imposed upon grazing."*

* Circular of the Government of India in the Department of Revenue and Agriculture dated 31st October, 1894.

Doubtless it is more troublesome to cut the grass, than to send the cattle to graze in the forests, but the damage done by cattle, particularly in districts with a dry climate, is out of all proportion to the value of the fodder obtained. The people would be better off, if they relied more upon stall feeding. Grass preserves, where cattle fodder is cut to be stacked and which are rigorously closed against grazing until the grass has been cut, are not unknown in India, they are found even in districts with a moist climate. All around Simla in the North-West Himalaya these grass preserves (ghasnis) on the hillslopes may be distinguished in spring and summer at a distance by their fresh green tint. Generally they are the common property of the village, they are carefully demarcated, all loose stones are removed, and no cattle are allowed inside. At the close of the rains the area is divided among the householders into long narrow strips, generally running down the slope of the hill. Each shareholder cuts the grass on his plot and stacks it for winter use. In autumn, after the hay has been removed, cattle are sometimes allowed to graze on these lands. In the dry climate of Ajmere and Merwara, to throw open the protected areas to cattle, except when necessary in seasons of drought, means, that the forest growth upon them does not improve, and that, when their help is wanted, these lands will to a great extent be found barren and useless. In spite of these concessions, the Commissioner reports, that all forest restrictions are thoroughly disliked by the people generally. Added to this a theory had been put forward by the Engineer officers in charge of the tanks, that these would fill better, if the hills were bare. True, trees and shrubs take up a portion of the water which falls, but they also check evaporation of the water not thus taken up, and they prevent the washing down of silt, and in many cases they facilitate the formation of springs and small rivulets which feed the tanks, not suddenly, but steadily.

The result has not been what it might have been, and what was hoped it would be, when the Forest Regulation of 1874 was passed. In many other places reserves for the production of grass have been established by officers of the Civil and Forest Department, but nowhere has action been taken on a scale commensurate with the great interests at stake. For it must never be forgotten: seasons of drought will always be one of the difficulties of India, and in the districts with a dry climate, in Rajputana, the Punjab, and part of the North-West Provinces as well as in the Deccan, the provision of cattle fodder in seasons of drought has hitherto been the chief difficulty.

The papers tell us, that during the present distressing scarcity, the result of the short Monsoon of 1896, all forests in the affected districts have been opened to grazing, wherever such was necessary. And it is most satisfactory to learn, that wherever forests had been effectively protected, they are now in a position to furnish an abundance of cattle fodder. The Hon[ble] A. T. Shuttleworth, Conservator of Forests Central Circle, Bombay, the first forest officer who has had the honour of being appointed a Member of the Legislative Council, himself directs the operations for providing cattle fodder from the forests throughout the Presidency. These operations mainly consist in cutting grass and pressing it in 80 lb. bales, which are sold at cost price at depôts all over the affected districts. He has made cartroads into the forests, to bring out the grass, and has several hundred presses at work. In previous famines the provision of cattle fodder on an adequate scale was, as a rule, impossible. Thanks to the more complete network of railways, to a good system of organization, but mainly to the improved condition of the forests, that difficulty seems, in the Bombay Presidency at least, to have been overcome, and Mr. Shuttleworth now has the great satisfaction to reap the reward of his indomitable energy, in demarcating and endeavouring efficiently to protect, forest areas of sufficient extent in the different districts of Bombay, when the Indian Forest Act was applied to that Presidency in 1878.

Evil Effects of Denudation.

In the Hoshiarpur district of the Punjab the Siwalik range of hills stretches from the Bias to the Sutlej river in a south-easterly direction. These hills consist of conglomerate, a very soft friable sandstone, alternating with strata of loam and clay. Formerly these hills were fairly well wooded. In 1846 they became British territory, the consequence was a rapid increase of population, a great demand for wood and charcoal in the fertile plains of the Hoshiarpur and the adjoining Jalandhar district, and the influx of a floating population of graziers with large herds of cattle. The result was complete denudation of the hills. The loose soil, no longer protected by vegetation, was washed down, broad rivers of sand spread into the plains below, and the end has been, that fields and gardens of 914 villages, once prosperous, are now covered with sand, which has laid waste upwards of 70,000 acres of fertile lands. This rich district is now traversed by numerous parallel sandy belts, cut out of the fertile and crop bearing area, and now rendered worthless.

These destructive rivers of sand, known as the Chos of Hoshiarpur, were first prominently brought to notice in 1878 by Mr. Coldstream, then Deputy Commissioner of the Hoshiarpur district, and by Mr. B. H. Baden-Powell, at that time Conservator of Forests, Punjab. The only remedy possible is to attack the evil at its source, to place these hills under strict protection, to prevent fires, to exclude goats and to regulate grazing and cutting. This portion of the country has a moist climate, a rainfall of 35 to 40 inches, as against 20 to 22 inches in Ajmere and Merwara. Experience has shown in the Saharanpur Siwaliks, that the protection of 4 years only is sufficient to clothe the sides of denuded hills, with coppice shoots, seedling trees, grass and herbs, and thus to control the streams draining them, which formerly used to cover the land below with sand and gravel. Otherwise the difficulty is here the same, as in Ajmere. At settlement the waste lands were made over to the villages. But here as in Ajmere, though the State has relinquished its rights, the lands have not become private but have remained public property, they are the common lands of the villages. And the State has not only the right but the duty to interfere, when the management of these lands endangers the prosperity of the country. In 1883 Mr. McA. Moir was deputed to investigate the subject. He submitted definite and practical proposals, but no action was taken. In 1887 a French Forest Officer, M. Uselle, visited India, and examined one of these torrents of sand near Hoshiarpur. The spectacle to him was simply a matter of astonishment. In France, he remarked,* " we should not content ourselves with looking at "the evil and complaining about it, we should take instant "measures to stamp it out, we should act and not talk." Volumes have been written upon the Chos of Hoshiarpur, but no useful action has as yet been taken. As in Ajmere, it will probably be necessary to have recourse to legislation, and the people who live upon these hills, and who graze their cattle there, will for a time necessarily be put to some inconvenience. The whole of the land however would not be taken up at once, but gradually, and in the moister climate of this district, tracts with good soil and favourably situated, if matters were properly managed, would within a few years be fit to yield ample cattle fodder.

Similar difficulties have presented themselves, and have been successfully met in other countries. In France the deterioration of the slopes in many parts of the Alps, the Cevennes and the Pyrenees, the result of reckless clearances and excessive grazing, had long ago manifested itself in the formation of torrents, the destruction of hill pastures, of fertile fields and meadows in the valleys, which were covered by masses of stones, gravel and sand, brought down by these torrents. A further result of these calamities were disastrous floods in the rivers. The inundations of 1856 and 1859 were extremely severe, extensive damage

---

* Indian Forester, Vol. XIII., p. 525.

was done all over the country, embankments and other works of protection had proved useless, and the feeling had become general, that the evil must be attacked at its source. In 1860 and 1864* two Laws were passed, which empowered the Government to carry out the necessary works on lands belonging to towns, villages, public institutions and private proprietors, to fix unstable slopes by weirs, retaining walls and other structures, and wherever the ground was sufficiently stable, to cover it with turf or to plant it up. These laws were passed under the Second Empire. Action was taken with great energy, and large sums were spent annually upon these operations. At the outset complaints were numerous, but gradually the beneficial effect of these measures made itself felt and progress became steady and satisfactory. Under the Republic agitation against the old laws recommenced, and after protracted deliberations in the Senate and in the Chamber of Deputies, a fresh law on the same subject was passed in 1882,† considerably curtailing the powers of Government. Under this law the taking up of a new area to be operated upon must be sanctioned by a special law in each case. On communal lands however Government can require the regulation of grazing, and all lands, whether communal or private property, that may require such protection, may be closed against cattle, equitable compensation being paid to the parties concerned. In 1889 the aggregate area successfully operated upon under these laws amounted to 469,000 acres. This however is only a small portion of the total area requiring special protection, and under the law of 1882 operations have become much more expensive. Fortunately a movement has commenced in these mountainous regions, gradually to substitute horned cattle for sheep and goats, as the cheese made from cows' milk pays better.

* Loi du 28 Juillet 1860 sur le reboisement des montagnes. Loi du 8 Juin 1864 sur le gazonnement des montagnes.
† Loi du 4 Avril, 1882, relative à la restauration et à la conservation des terrains en montagne.

This movement is strongly supported by Government, for sheep and goats do infinitely more mischief than cattle.

The good effect of these measures has already brought its reward, and though progress has not been as rapid as was originally hoped, the condition of the mountainous districts has greatly improved.

In Austria and Switzerland operations have been carried on in a similar manner and with very marked success.

Most fortunately for the Hoshiarpur district the Government of India have quite lately decided to take action. In referring to the regulation and restriction of grazing in the Siwaliks of the North-Western Provinces, the Government write (2nd July 1896): " In the hills of the Hoshiarpur " district in the Punjab, the unrestricted cutting of fuel, " the grazing of buffaloes and browsing animals have " resulted in the almost total disappearance of wood and " grass, and in the most serious injury to the highly " cultivated plains below; for the protection of which " costly measures are now to be undertaken, the necessity " for which might have been avoided, had timely regulation " been possible."

The Ratnagiri district on the western coast, south of Bombay, is hilly, but the hills are almost bare to the crest of the ghats. The effect of denudation has shown itself by the silting up of the streams which rise in the ghat mountains, and run a short course to the sea; some of these rivers formerly were important for trade, now they are only navigable for small boats. Excepting the plains, there is hardly a district in India, in the moist as well as in the dry regions where the evil effects of denudation are not visible.

As population augments, as more forest is cleared for cultivation, the difficulty of taking measures to combat these evils increases. These measures unavoidably, in India as in Europe, involve a certain amount of inconvenience to the present generation, and such interference is felt as a grievance. What is now commonly urged by well meaning but short sighted public officers as " a more lenient forest policy" will, if the Indian Empire remains under British rule, and population continues to increase as at present, carry its own punishment in the shape of serious calamities. In the summer of 1893 the drought in central Germany was extremely severe, over large areas the corn withered before ripening, the crop of hay was extremely scanty, cattle were sold at less than one fourth their usual price, and the cattle which the peasants retained must have perished, had it not been for the forests, chiefly those belonging to the State and to villages. These forests yielded grass and leaves in abundance, but they would not have been in a condition to afford this help, had they been opened to grazing and had they not been rigidly protected, in the teeth of the oft expressed serious discontent among the agricultural classes. During the excited times of 1848, when the relaxation of all restrictions was everywhere demanded in Germany, several villages in the Kingdom of Würtemberg demanded permission to divide their communal forests among the householders of the village. In a weak moment the Government consented, the forests were divided and sold. The proceeds soon disappeared, for 1848 was a year of excited popular assemblies, of drinking and carousing in that part of the country. These villages I visited in 1865, and the people complained bitterly of their poverty. The villages in the vicinity, that had put up with the restrictions, which good forest management demands, were prosperous and happy. No communal taxes, for the steady annual forest income paid for roads, lighting, schools and churches, and in addition yielded to each householder firewood in abundance for the winter, and timber for the repair of their houses.

The Dehra Dùn Forest School.

The extended employment of natives in the forests was urged by me in 1868. In a Report dated 28th July I said : "Ultimately it is hoped, that a large proportion of native forest officers for the higher appointments may be available.

It cannot be sufficiently urged, that, unless the practice of rational forest management becomes the common property of the natives of this country, the permanence of the measures now initiated and their ultimate beneficial effects will remain uncertain."* Referring to this Report Sir Stafford Northcote (the late Earl of Iddesleigh), then Secretary of State for India, wrote in a despatch to the Governor-General : " I am glad to perceive that Dr. Brandis appreciates the great importance of interesting and employing the natives of India in forest administration, a most important step, as he observes, to the stability of the measures taken with that view."†

The plan which at that time I had framed in order to realize these objects, was as follows : The Officers of the protective and executive Branch of the forest service should all be natives of India, while the officers of the controlling branch should be Englishmen, who had received their professional training in the forests of France or Germany. At that time a sharp division between Controlling and Executive officers was not possible. The officers in charge of Forest divisions had necessarily charge of the executive work in the forest ranges included within their division. But eventually, as the management of these forest ranges became more intensive and as the growing revenue permitted such outlay, Rangers would be appointed as executive Officers. These should all be natives of India, they should receive a thorough professional training and should in case of distinguished service have the prospect of promotion to the controlling branch, and of rising to high appointments. At that time I held, what I hold much more strongly at the present moment, that few measures were more likely to secure the maintenance of British Rule in India, than a more extended employment of Natives in responsible positions in the public service. And I considered, that the

---

* Parliamentary Return on Forest Conservancy, Part I., India, 1871, p. 393.
† Ibidem, p. 405.

Forest Department was one of those, in which, without any political risk, the highest appointments might be filled by Natives. In those days I regarded the arrangements for the professional training of young Englishmen as a measure of temporary character, and the establishment eventually of Forest Schools in India as the main object to be aimed at.

At an early date I had fixed upon Dehra Dùn at the foot of the North-West Himalaya, as the seat of the future Indian Forest School, and I did, what I could, by personal influence with the local officers, to get a good system of management introduced in the Dùn forests, in those outside the Siwaliks in the Saharanpur district, and those in Jaunsar and the adjoining leased forests of the North West Himalaya. From the commencement I held, that the teaching at the Indian Forest School must be mainly practical and that in order to make this possible, large areas of well-managed forest must be attached to the School. Fortunately the establishment of a large Military Cantonment at Chakrata in 1869, with an annual consumption of 312,000 cub. ft. of stacked firewood, necessitated the preparation of a working plan for the forests that were to supply that wood. Accordingly I prepared, in November, 1874 and April 1875, with the assistance of the local forest officers, a preliminary working plan, intended to provide for the needful cuttings until 1878. Similar work was done in the other forests, which I intended should eventually form the School Forests.

But the idea of a Forest School for Native Forest rangers at that time found little favour with the leading authorities in India. By many the professional training of young Englishmen for Forest Service was still regarded as a needless, nay as a mischievous attempt at over-refinement. A forester must be a keen sportsman, must have a strong constitution and plenty of common sense. That is all that can possibly be needed in India. To establish a Forest School, in order to give a professional training to Native Forest Rangers, seemed an Utopian beginning. By that time the forests had been made subordinate to a newly created Department of the Government of India of Land Revenue and Agriculture, and my Chief, the Secretary in that Department, Mr. A. O. Hume, C.B., was strongly opposed to the measure. At last in 1878, at the end of a long and severe fight, I carried my point with the assistance of several Members of the Government of India, who had confidence in my judgment.

Sanction however was only given on condition, that no additional outlay should be required. This necessitated arrangements which were imperfect and in some instances faulty through excessive economy. Under these circumstances the success of the undertaking entirely depended upon the person selected as Director. Major F. Bailey of the Royal Engineers, had joined the Forest Department in 1871, and had done excellent service, both while in charge of the Dehra Dùn Division, as well as subsequently in organizing a special branch of the Service for the topographical survey of the forests, which has furnished at a very moderate outlay excellent maps of the State Forests in several provinces. Under Major (afterwards Colonel) Bailey as Conservator of the School Forests, the area of which now aggregates 516,000 acres, and Director of the Forest School, the management of the forests was steadily improved, the revenue increased, and this made it possible, gradually to strengthen the Staff of Instructors. The leading principle was slow but steady progress.

In 1881 the first successful students left the School, three with the Rangers' and two with the Sub. Asst. Conservators' certificate. Subsequently a lower class was established, in which only a forester's Certificate could be obtained. Altogether in 1895, 355 professionally trained men, all Natives of India, the majority belonging to Indian races, had left the School, of whom 273 had obtained the Certificate as Forest Rangers (three of them as Sub. Asst. Conservators) while 82 obtained the Forester's certificate. The students of the lower class, those who prepare for the forester's certificate, come from those provinces in Northern and Central India, where Hindustani is commonly spoken, and to these instruction is given in that language, while the Candidates for the Ranger's Certificate are taught in English. Handbooks in English and in Hindustani for the students of the School have been published and are under preparation. In the Bombay Presidency arrangements have been made at the Poona College of Science, to give Candidates for the Forest Service instruction in forestry and natural sciences.

Working Plans controlled by Inspector-General of Forests.

Attention has before been drawn to the fact, that the first attempt to regulate the working of forests by a working plan was made in Pegu in 1856. In later years the writer of this paper was able to prepare preliminary working plans for several districts in other provinces, and Dr. Schlich, while Conservator of Forests in Bengal, prepared working plans for some forests in that province, Obviously, since trees take 100 years and more to attain a marketable size, working plans are indispensable, and regular working-plans must sketch out forest operations for a lengthy period. The work of preparing working plans for the more important forests in all provinces could not be attempted, until a sufficient number of professionally trained officers with sufficiently long experience of the country were available. Dr. Schlich has the great merit of having started this business on a large scale. In order to enable him to control this important work, an Assistant Inspector-General was appointed and the powers of the Inspector-General of Forests were considerably enlarged. All working plans, previous to being sanctioned by the Local Government were submitted for his approval. In other respects also the position of the chief forest officer was greatly strengthened. He was invested with the control of the forest school and forest survey and was authorized, upon professional matters, to correspond directly with Conservators of Forests.

In the early days of forest administration the main point aimed at was, not to centralize but to throw the responsibility of forest administration entirely upon Local Governments. In those days it was better that the Inspector General of Forests should have no official authority and that he should be merely the adviser of the Government of India and of Local Governments. His chief duty therefore consisted in visits to the forests in different provinces in company with the local officers. If he succeeded in securing their assent to his own ideas, and if the Local Government approved of his suggestions, well and good. In provinces where this was not the case, the local officers had to be left to their own devices. Progress under these circumstances was unequal in the different provinces. Hence the greater powers, which were given to the Inspector General of Forests, after Dr. Schlich had succeeded me, marked an important step in advance. At first sight it may be regarded as a retrograde step in the direction of centralization. This however was not the case, for by that time the principle of placing Divisional forest officers under the orders of the Civil district officer, effectually guarded against undue centralization.

One of the most important results of the Dehra Dún Forest School has been, that several native officers, who had received their professional training at that school, are now being employed on the preparation of working plans for important forests, and that their work compares favourably with the work of Englishmen educated on the continent of Europe or at Cooper's Hill College. The present Inspector-General of Forests in his Review of Forest administration in British India for 1894-95 states: "There are many trained Rangers of pure native extraction who yield nothing to anyone." This is a most satisfactory result, and I must claim the indulgence of the reader still for a few further remarks to show, how this result may be utilized, to remove some of the difficulties under which Indian Forestry at present is labouring.

The Increase of Population necessitates good Forest Management.

Within the 10 years which intervened between the Census of 1881 and 1891, the population of the British provinces (without Upper Burma) has increased by 19,365,000* or nearly two millions a year. But not only has the population increased in numbers, it has also increased in wealth. The consumption of forest produce per head of the population is steadily increasing. In towns and villages the people build better houses, requiring more timber and bamboos. In certain forest tracts the direction of the timber trade has of late years entirely changed. From North Kanara formerly the export of timber was all seawards, and fortunately it was not of great importance and had not exhausted the forests. The export inland was trifling. Since however the Civil war in America, after 1860, had stimulated the cultivation of cotton in the inland districts, a large demand for timber and bamboos for the cotton producing districts of the Southern Maratha country has sprung up and since that time the chief export of timber from the Kanara forests goes in that direction. Similar changes in the lines of timber export have taken place elsewhere in many places. The rapid construction, within the last 40 years, of railways, canals and public buildings of all descriptions has created large demands for timber and wood.

The consumption of sugar which, apart from tobacco, is the chief luxury among the native population, is augmenting rapidly, and the cultivation of sugar cane is increasing on a large scale. In his working plan of the Gorakhpur forests (1893) Lala Har Swarup explains, that wood fuel finds a ready market now in that district for brick burning, the manufacture of Saltpetre and for Sugar

---

* 1891 : 221,173,000 less 2,947,000 = 218,226,000
1881   198,861,000
                                                   ───────────
                                                    19,365,000

factories, which in that year numbered 299 in the district. Those forests I visited in 1864, they contain little valuable timber, and revenue from the sale of firewood I regarded as hopeless at that time. Keshavanand, another of the older Native Forest officers trained at Dehra Dún, in his working plan of the Charda forest in Oudh (1894) proposes to treat this forest with the object of producing a maximum amount of fuel and small timber, all of which can, he adds, be disposed of either locally or to the railway. This forest I had visited repeatedly, in 1863, 1875 and 1880, and the difficulty always was want of sufficient demand for the inferior wood it produces.

There is however no necessity for going into detail. The steady growth of forest revenue proves the steadily increasing consumption of forest produce in the British provinces.

During the 3 years ending	Revenue. R.	Mean annual Expenditure. R.	Surplus. R.
1874-75	6,352,000.	4,363,000.	1,989,000.
1884-85	10,267,000.	6,546,000.	3,721,000.
1894-95	16,948,000.	9,206,000.	7,742,000.

The export of forest produce beyond India, chiefly Lac, Cutch, Myrobalans and Teak timber, is insignificant. The Teak timber exported from Rangoon and Maulmein 40 years ago amounted to 86,000 tons (at 50 cub. ft.) annually, nearly the whole of which in those days was sent to Great Britain and North America. During the 5 years ending with 1894-95 the quantity exported from these ports had risen to 188,100 tons, but of this quantity only about 45,000 tons were sent to countries outside India. The bulk of the Teak timber exported from the Burma ports now goes to Bombay, Madras and Calcutta, as the forests of the western peninsula are not sufficient to meet the requirements of the older portions of the British Indian Empire. The growth of Revenue therefore, both gross and net revenue, is a true index of the growing consumption of forest produce in India.

It is this steady growth of the population and this steady

growth of the requirements of the people in regard to forest produce, that necessitates a regular management of the limited forest area available to meet these requirements. The aim should be, to produce the largest quantity of timber, bamboos and other produce, on the smallest area possible.

Extension of Cultivation by relinquishing Land in the remote Timber Forests.

A remarkable Resolution on the subject of Forest policy by the Government of India of 19 October 1894, which was published in the Gazette of India and in the Indian Forester,* justly mentions the pressure of the population upon the soil as one of the greatest difficulties, that India has to face, and adds : " that application of the soil must generally be preferred, which will support the largest numbers in proportion to the area." That resolution establishes the following classes of forests, being State property in India, while acknowledging that some forests may occupy intermediate positions and that parts of one and the same forest may fall under different heads :

(a) Forests, the preservation of which is essential on climatic or physical grounds.
(b) Forests, which afford a supply of valuable timber for commercial purposes.
(c) Minor forests.
(d) Pasture lands.

The second class comprises the forests situated in the more remote thinly populated and mostly mountainous districts, with a moist climate. They produce Teak, Sál, Deodar and other valuable trees. Regarding them the Resolution says, that " wherever an effective demand for culturable land exists, and can only be supplied from forest areas, the land should ordinarily be relinquished without hesitation." That this might be done, has been recognized from the commencement of forest demarcation in India. In

---

* Indian Forester, XX., p. 414.

those districts, where there still existed a large extent of forest at the disposal of Government, very extensive areas were deliberately demarcated, in the hope, that after these forests had been brought into good condition, villages might be established in suitable positions within these forests. The indispensable condition however of this being possible is, so to improve their productiveness, as to secure the same annual supply of forest produce from a smaller area. This end can only be attained by strict protection and regular working. At the time this project was pronounced as fanciful. Localities within the forests, it was said, are uninhabitable, the people settled there will perish of fever. The reply was, that in the wildest forest regions of India we constantly come across evidence, that the land at one time had been under cultivation, fruit trees, ruins of large buildings and terraces of old fields. There is very little of what may justly be called virgin forest in India. Where people once lived and prospered, there they can live and prosper again.

So far regarding the establishment of permanent settlements in the heart of the more remote forests, in order to provide for the surplus population of the open country. It must not however be overlooked, that the separation between forest and the lands allotted to such settlements must be sharp and absolute. A liberal allotment of land must be made to the settlers, but no rights to grazing or other user in the forest must be granted. For it cannot be sufficiently urged, that in forests, which are not completely under the proprietor's control, in which other persons exercise rights of grazing or cutting wood, regular management becomes very difficult.

Paramount Importance of Minor Forests and Pasture Lands.

An entirely different matter is the alienation of lands included in forests comprised under the two last classes, those which are situated in the open country, minor forests and pasture lands. The relinquishment for purposes of cultivation of such forest lands is specially encouraged in the Resolution of 19 October 1894, on the ground of these classes of forests being less valuable than the timber forests. The maintenance and the good management of these minor forests however is of much greater moment for the welfare of the agricultural population in the open country than the maintenance of the so-called valuable timber forests, which are mostly situated in remote mountainous regions. This is the point, which to this present day does not seem to be understood in India.

One of the most densely populated districts under the Lieutenant Governor of the North Western provinces and Oudh is Gorakhpur. This district has already been mentioned. The State Forests here are scattered over the northern and north-eastern portion of the district, there are 14 detached blocks, in size varying from 55 to 26,500 acres. The ground is flat and, though the principal tree is Sál, the timber is small, and these lands would properly be classed under minor forests. They are interlaced with grass lands, likewise included within forest limits, which may be designated as pasture lands. It will be convenient to compare this district with one of the States of the German Empire, the Kingdom of Saxony.

	Area Square miles.	Population.	Population per sq. mile.	State Forest sq. miles.	Percentage of State Forest to total area.
Gorakhpur	4,576	2,994,000	654	172	3·8 %
Saxony	5,750	3,783,000	658	652	11·3 %

Besides its State Forests the Kingdom of Saxony has 846 square miles of forests, mostly belonging to private proprietors. These also are managed on the same system and as efficiently as those belonging to the State. In Saxony therefore 26% of the total area are occupied by well managed forests, as against 3·8% in Gorakhpur, for the private forests here are insignificant.

The population of Saxony is partly manufacturing, partly agricultural, but had the country not so large an area under well managed forests, it could not possibly maintain its large population. As it is, the forest area is not sufficient for its requirements. Large quantities of timber are imported from Bohemia, partly by land, partly floated down the river Elbe, to provide sawmills, paper pulp factories and other industrial establishments with material. The difference in the condition of the two countries certainly is considerable. Less timber is required for house building and less firewood is consumed in the mild climate of Gorakhpur. But as already mentioned, there are considerable wood-consuming industries in the district. And this equally applies to the two adjoining districts, which, with Gorakhpur, form the Division of that name, Basti with 645 Souls on the Square mile and Azamgarh with 805. These two districts have no forest at all at present. The area under Sugar cane alone in these three districts in 1895 aggregated 201,161* acres and the manufacture of sugar consumes large quantities of firewood. In 1864, as already mentioned, a revenue from the sale of firewood seemed hopeless, now the whole produce sells readily. Gorakhpur has a mean annual rainfall of 49 inches, and the district is extremely fertile. Of the area under crops one half nearly are rice fields.

If peace is maintained in India, it will ere long be found, that in this district the forest area is much too small, and if not too late, efforts will then doubtless be made, to increase it. Fortunately, a large area of waste land, partly culturable, partly unfit for cultivation, is available, amounting in 1895 to 1,034 Square miles or 22·6% of the total area, and much of this is covered with grass, trees and brushwood. A most valuable reserve for the gradual extension of cultivation, but at present its produce is worth very little.

The difference between the two countries is this: In the Kingdom of Saxony 26% of the total area is forest efficiently managed, while 74% are cultivated, hardly an acre lying waste. Gorakhpur maintains about the same population on the Square mile. Of its area 73·6% are cultivated, 3·8%

* Agricultural Statistics of British India, 1890-91 to 1894-5, Calcutta, 1896, pages 149-151.

well managed forest and 22·6% are waste. In both cases, of the cultivated area, there are 0·72% acres per head of the population, but, while in Saxony the uncultivated area (26%) is well managed forest, every acre of which yields useful produce, in Gorakhpur 22·6% of the district is permitted to lie waste. True, these lands are used for grazing, and a little wood is cut here and there, but they do not yield what they might, if placed under proper management. Cattle fodder alone might be produced more abundantly on a much smaller area. Certainly, in the mild climate of Gorakhpur less firewood is required, than in the cold winters of Germany. But even here it would be prudent, before it is too late, seriously to consider, what portion of the waste should be added to the forest area, in order to make sufficient provision for this as well as for the adjoining forestless districts. So much will be clear from what has been stated, that even in a favourably situated district, like Gorakhpur, the point to be aimed at, is not to relinquish any portions of the forest area for the extension of cultivation, but rather to enlarge that forest area, and to diminish the unproductive area of waste lands. Afterwards, if it should be found necessary, to break up land for the plough, it will be found, that fields, which had been stocked with forest, are more fertile than the present barren waste.

The gigantic size of the British Indian Empire is fitly illustrated by the fact, that we have compared one of the larger States of the German Empire with one of the 49 districts in the North-West Provinces. It is also illustrated by the following comparison of the British provinces with the entire German Empire.

	Area square miles.	Population.	Population per square mile.	State Forests square miles.	Percentage of State forest to total area.
British provinces of India	964,993	221,173,000	229	74,271	7·7 %
German Empire	208,687	52,246,000	250	17,918	8·6 %

At first sight these two large countries, which maintain

nearly the same number on the Square mile, though they are widely different in regard to configuration of the country, climate, vegetation and the habits of its inhabitants, would seem to be nearly on a par in regard to Forest management. In reality however this is not the case. In the German Empire, as in the Kingdom of Saxony, the forests belonging to towns, villages, public institutions and private proprietors are as a rule as well managed as those of the State, and these aggregate 35,970 Square miles, so that the area of well managed forests amounts to 25·82% of the country. In the British provinces of India, besides the reserved forests entered in the above Statement, the returns include 7,090 Square miles of protected and 31,591 of unclassed State forests, but protection and management of these tracts is not such as to justify our taking them into account.

Establishment of Village Forests.

Besides these areas however, which are classed as forests in India, there are in each province large areas of waste, aggregating 390,000 Square miles, or considerably more than one third of the whole area. It has above been explained, that eventually it may be advisable, in the extensive and remote timber forests to establish villages and there to relinquish land for cultivation. At the same time however attempts must be made upon an adequate scale in each province, to improve the productiveness of these large areas of waste lands, and where the nature of the land tenure admits of it, to establish village forests. The formation of grass and fuel preserves has been the first step in this direction. To this class belong the reserves in Ajmere-Merwara. Attempts more or less successful have been made here and there in the North-West Provinces. The object is to produce heavier crops of firewood and grass in the open cultivated country. It has now been sufficiently established, that strict protection, aided by sowing and planting, during a number of years, longer or shorter, according to the climate, produces a covering of shrubs and grass and yields a crop of cattle fodder, which at first must be utilized by cutting, while afterwards cattle may be permitted to graze during certain seasons.

It is immaterial, which agency is employed in these operations. On the banks of Canals the Officers of the Irrigation Department look after these areas, elsewhere the work may be done by the Civil or Forest Officers. All I wish to say is, that there exists an agency of Officers specially trained for work of this kind, whom in most cases it may be found useful to employ. Native Forest rangers, who have received their professional education at Dehra Dùn, ought to be specially fitted for these undertakings, working under the direction of the Collector of the district.

It may be useful, once more to mention the Azamgarh district, which adjoins Gorakhpur on the South. A poor densely populated district with 805 souls on the Square mile. The area cultivated in 1894-95, together with regular fallows, amounted to 886,000 acres,* giving only 0·51 acre per head as against 0·72 acres in Gorakhpur and Basti. Fortunately however no less than 501,000 acres of crops were irrigated, a much larger percentage than in either of the two adjoining districts. Nevertheless the people are poor, living mostly from hand to mouth, and dwelling in miserable huts of dried mud. The waste lands aggregate 490,000 acres or 35% of the total area. But there are trees in the ravines (Butea and Acacia arabica). Here is a promising task for a skilful forester. There are special difficulties, extensive marshes and usar lands, impregnated with salt. The plan ought to be, to take up block after block and thus gradually to convert a portion of these waste lands into productive forest, the object being, at first to produce an abundant supply of firewood and cattle fodder, and eventually small wood, to enable the people to build

---

* Agricultural Statistics of British India 1890-91 to 1894-95. Calcutta, 1896, page 58.

better houses, and for agricultural implements. The first step must be, to make the waste land produce more than it does at present, and the second to give up from the improved waste land such portions, as may be suitable for the extension of cultivation.

In his Report on the improvement of Indian Agriculture, Dr. Voelcker justly urges the establishment on a larger scale of fuel and fodder reserves, for the primary purpose of supplying wood to take the place of cow dung as fuel. "If wood," he says,* "could be made to take the place of "dung for fuel, we should soon come to realize, that more "wood means more manure, that more manure means "heavier crops, and an increasing fertility of the soil."

With the view of an eventual development in this direction, clauses providing for the establishment of village forests were inserted in the Indian and Burma Forest Acts. Experience has shown in Germany, in France and in other countries of Europe, that municipal institutions develop in a healthy manner, where the municipalities have landed property. In the case of municipal forests it has in these countries been found expedient, to entrust the State with a supervision of their management. The necessity for such supervision is obvious, and should waste lands in India ever be transformed into village forests, the same plan will doubtless be followed.

Perhaps these ideas will be put aside as the outcome of Departmental zeal, which always trenches upon the traditions of the Native population, their cherished customs and privileges. But the British Nation has undertaken the responsibility for the millions inhabiting this huge Empire, that population is increasing rapidly and steadily. A long period of internal peace, security of persons and property, good government, the impartial administration of justice, the development of commerce, manufactures and agriculture, canals and other irrigation works, roads, railways, and, by

* Voelcker, Report on the Improvement of Indian Agriculture. London, 1893, p. 137.

no means least, schools and colleges—all this has brought about a tide of progress, which cannot now be stemmed. There is no help for it, whether the work is done by Departments of the public service or otherwise, the clock cannot be put back. But the blessings of progress will be valued more by the people, if they are not all dispensed by the hand of the Foreigner, if Natives themselves are the agents to a greater extent, than is the case at present, in the undertakings which contribute to their well being. A well planned system of making the waste lands in the different provinces more productive than they are at present, is one of the great points that should be aimed at. This work however ought as far as possible to be entrusted to Native agency.

The Difficulties of the Task must be faced.

All the world over people living in the forests or in their vicinity, feel the commencement of strict protection as a hardship, howsoever considerate the settlement of forest rights may have been. Old customs are more comfortable, the interests of the present moment more powerful, than care for the future. Not everywhere may it be possible, by giving them opportunities of earning money through forest work, and by supplying their wants in a liberal manner, to gain the good will of these people, as has been the case with the Karens in Burma.

This however has been possible in other provinces also, and as an instance I will quote the following passage from a Review of the Berar Forest Report for 1892-93 by Colonel Kenneth Mackenzie, the Commissioner of that province. In 1865 Mackenzie as Assistant Commissioner, acting under the orders of Colonel Pearson, then Conservator of Forests Central Provinces and Berar, organized forest business in Berar. In 1893 he writes as follows: " Intimately connected with the welfare of the forests is the " prosperity of the people in and immediately around our " reserves, their well being, on which follows their good will,

"depends on the wise adjustment of our forest concessions
"to their necessities. Luckily our position, especially in
"the Melghat, enabled us to be liberal, with the result, that
"the people in the hill tracts are well affected towards us.
"They practically form an unpaid protective force, of great
"value, in addition to our own staff. Without their ready
"and willing assistance, our great success in fire conser-
"vancy would have been impossible."

The real strength of the gigantic British Indian Empire consists in the prosperity and contentment of its inhabitants. The British Nation may well be proud of having accomplished this—of having established a strong, just and considerate Government among the numerous nationalities of British India. At first sight it seems an impossible task, to secure the contentment of the people, while interfering with their habits, however great the future benefits may be, that will result from such interference. Nowhere in the world has there been real and important progress without temporary dissatisfaction. In India also means must be found, that will enable Government to provide for the future welfare of the steadily growing population, in spite of the temporary discontent its action may cause.

Native Forest Officers must be employed in responsible Appointments.

A minute written by Sir Thomas Munro, when Governor of Madras, on 31 December 1824, on the employment of Natives in the public service, suggests the measures which should be taken. He writes: "All offices that can be held "by natives without danger to our power, might with advantage be left to them"* and further on follow remarks to the following effect. "To improve the character of the "natives, we must open the road to wealth and honour and "public employment."

The best plan which can be suggested, in order to mitigate

* Sir Thomas Munro, Bart., K.C.B., by Sir Alexander J. Arbuthnot, Vol. II. London, 1881, page 319.

the friction which is the unavoidable consequence of strict protection and a regular system of working, is to employ as many competent and professionally trained Native forest officers, not only in subordinate but also in responsible positions. It is not maintained, that Native Forest Officers will necessarily be more considerate than Englishmen. But in any case it cannot be said against them, that they lack the perfect knowledge, the deep insight into and the sympathy with the feelings and prejudices of Asiatics. One point is certain, they will be able, with greater force to insist upon the advantages which the people actually derive from well managed and efficiently protected forests, more abundant and permanent supply of forest produce, heavier dew on the fields in the vicinity, and shelter against scorching winds. The larger the number of natives employed in responsible positions in the forests, the more forestry will cease to have the character of an exotic plant, or a foreign artificially fostered institution. In order however to attain this object, it will be necessary greatly to strengthen the Staff of the School forests attached to the Dehra Dún School, and eventually to establish similar schools in other parts of the country, particularly in Burma.

Against these proposals it may be urged, that in Ajmere-Merwara the chief forest officers have during the last five or six years been natives of India of Asiatic extraction, and that nevertheless the majority of the reserves have been annually opened to grazing. This however was the Commissioner's order. An English Officer might perhaps have remonstrated with greater energy. But this does not weaken the strength of the present argument, that the more extended employment of Native Forest Officers in responsible positions, will make it easier for Government, to do its duty, with due regard to the future development of the British Indian Empire.

The measure here advocated must not be expected to yield great results at once. If decided upon, it must be carried out cautiously but steadily. The aim should be, gradually, in a few carefully selected districts, say in Berar or the Central Provinces, to fill all appointments with pure natives of India, and when this has proved a success, to proceed further. It will be a great point gained, when the first Native is appointed to the post of Conservator of Forests in Berar or in one of the Forest Circles of the Central Provinces. There is at present an Imperial Forest Service which is recruited from Cooper's Hill and a Provincial Service which is recruited from Dehra Dùn, and for Bombay from the Poona College of Science. Under existing orders members of the Provincial Forest Service can rise to the rank of Extra Deputy Conservator on 600 Rupees a month, but when the measures here advocated have been adopted, their prospects must, as a matter of course, be improved. Professional education must lead to an honourable and paying career. This once clearly established and publicly known, desirable and promising Native candidates will not be wanting, and upon the Indian Forest Schools will then mainly rest the duty of preparing men for forest work in India. However, the difficulties are not slight, and it is best to face them. In the Review of the Berar Forest Report previously quoted, Colonel Kenneth Mackenzie says : " There is very great difficulty in getting " physically fit and suitably educated young men now to " enter the ranger's grade, and every body who is " acquainted with the facts in the background, will agree " that a potent cause for this is the comparatively poorer " prospects, that such men at present have in the forests, as " compared with openings in other Departments. Conse- " quently it will certainly pay Government directly and " indirectly to improve their position. I do not think that " the hard work, the loneliness, the sickness, that these " men have to face, comes home in any thing like the " reality to those ultimately responsible for their welfare, as " it does to those who, like myself, are continuously brought " into intimate relation with facts. It fell to me, as " Assistant Commissioner in 1866, nearly 28 years ago, to

"select and demarcate our main reserves and to start,
"under the direction of Colonel George Pearson, what is
"now the Berar Forest Department—and of all the men I
"then enlisted, with one or two exceptions all young men
"of excellent physique, and locally acclimatized, but two
"now survive."

Another difficulty is adverted to by Mr. E. P. Dansey, an excellent officer of long experience. As Conservator of the Central Circle North West Provinces he wrote in his Report for 1894-95: "The most unprofitable of all sub-
"ordinate forest officers is the townbred school boy
"educated at Government expense in the rudiments of his
"profession, and who has had no long previous experience
"of jungle life, jungle tribes and jungle conditions generally."

These extracts indicate some of the breakers ahead. When the Forest School was started, it was laid down as a rule, that no student should be received, who had not proved his fitness for the forests by several years' work as a volunteer or as a forest guard. This rule it has apparently not been possible to maintain. So much however is certain, no students of the desirable classes will present themselves, unless they can look forward with certainty to good prospects of advancement.

Something has already been accomplished in Native States in this direction. A considerable number of smaller and a few larger States have imitated the example of the British Government, they have organized the administration of their forests, and in several instances men, who had received their professional training at Dehra Dùn, have been placed at the head. Mysore has a completely organized Forest Department. The present Conservator is Colonel Campbell Walker, formerly Senior Conservator of Forests, Madras, but under him are 14 Divisional Officers, all natives of India, and most of them natives of the Mysore State. In the Jammu and Kashmir State, Forest administration is making very good progress under Mr. McDonell, the Conservator of Forests. In the large Rajput States of

Marwar and Jaipur the Conservators of forests have from the commencement been Native Gentlemen trained at Dehra Dùn, and they have done remarkably well in that position. If forest service, be it in British territory or in Native States, once comes to be recognised as offering an honourable career, that may, as the reward of honesty, skill and energy, lead to high and well paid appointments, forestry will become naturalized in India and will cease to be looked upon as an attempt to introduce Foreign ideas and Foreign practices.

These plans are not new. Attempts to appoint Natives of India to responsible posts in the Forest Department were made many years ago, long before the Dehra Dùn School was established. These attempts have failed, because they were ordered to be made suddenly, and without the needful forethought. The measures here advocated must be allowed to develop slowly, but steadily, towards the point aimed at.

The proposals here made, gradually to employ Natives in responsible positions of the Indian Forest Department, have been made on one condition, and this condition is absolute, viz., that they have received an ample, thorough, practical, and theoretical training in their profession. Several times of late years the attempt has been made, to alter the constitution of the Dehra Dùn Forest School, and to remove the School forests from the Director's control. The Director of the School is and must be Conservator of the School Forests. This large forest area must be entirely under his control, establishments for the management and protection of it must be provided upon a liberal scale, the Divisional and Executive Officers, the Deputy Conservators and Rangers of the School forests must all be picked men. If this principle is not maintained, the employment of men trained at the School in responsible positions, is out of the question. Nay more is required. The Cooper's Hill forest students now most properly spend a considerable part of their time in Germany.

One of the advantages of this arrangement is, that it enables them, while in India, to remain in touch with the progress of forestry in Germany. No officer, who aspires to the high position of Conservator of forests, ought to be ignorant of what goes on in his profession in those countries of Europe, where it has attained its greatest perfection. A large number of young men from Japan are now in Germany, studying at forest schools, at Universities and other institutions. If Dehra Dùn is maintained and strengthened as it ought to be, it will hereafter come to be considered, how to enable Native Forest Officers, who have distinguished themselves in actual service, and who are anxious to rise further, to spend some time in the Forests of Germany. There they will find, that the villages, which own well managed communal forests, are prosperous, although now and then they may complain of the restrictions, which a good system of management unavoidably imposes. What Indian Forest Officers will learn in this respect in Germany, will be really useful to them in India.

Fanciful ideas, the reader may say, some indeed may call them Utopian. Thus was designated in 1860 the attempt, to work the Pegu forests on Government account, and to ensure from them a permanent and increasing yield of Teak timber. Fanciful and impossible was pronounced in 1865 the attempt to protect the forests against the annual Jungle fires. When in 1867 the professional education of young Englishmen was started in France and Germany, and when in 1878 the Dehra Dùn Forest School for Native students was established, these undertakings were regarded by many as useless and preposterous. We will comfort ourselves with the hope, that the employment of Native Forest Officers in responsible, nay in high positions, will some day be recognized as the only proper course to pursue.

THE END.

CPSIA information can be obtained
at www.ICGtesting.com
Printed in the USA
LVHW081413010820
661578LV00046B/353